WHATEVER *happened* TO DINNER?

"I rejoiced to see *Whatever Happened to Dinner?* by Melodie Davis. I rejoiced even more as I read the book and hope it will be a great encouragement and resource for families. The author loads the book with helpful suggestions and illustrations from life and Scripture, and with practical ideas as to how it can be done today. The family meal can still be the family's finest hour."
—John M. Drescher, author of *Seven Things Children Need*

"In her creative style, Melodie Davis calls us to meaningful family times as well as to community hospitality. Eating together is a universally recognized expression of friendship and peace. This book offers a good place to start— regular family meals, cultivating togetherness, and an extensive variety of recipes to help make it happen. Come to dinner, one and all."
—Myron S. Augsburger, President Emeritus of Eastern Mennonite University

"*Whatever Happened to Dinner?* gives a very nice assortment of recipes that cater to the trends of today's young people, plus ideas for entertaining when our teenagers invite their friends over to eat. It's also a real eye-opener to the many positive influences acquired by sharing at family mealtimes. This book will certainly be an inspiration to anyone wanting to hand valuable traditions of the past to the next generation."
—Esther H. Shank, author of *Mennonite Country-Style Recipes & Kitchen Secrets*

"*Whatever Happened to Dinner?* seeks to inspire rather than lament. People are busy, families are complicated, and our food system is troublesome. That's the world we live in. Let's sit down to dinner and, in that daily act, find ways to bring as much sense, joy, and redemption to our world as we can."
—Pam Peters-Pries, food columnist for *Purpose* magazine

Part of the Third Way Collection

WHATEVER *happened* TO DINNER?

Recipes and Reflections for Family Mealtime

• • • • • • • • • • • • • • • •

Melodie M. Davis
with Jodi Nisly Hertzler and Carmen Wyse

Herald Press
Scottdale, Pennsylvania
Waterloo, Ontario

Library of Congress Cataloging-in-Publication Data
Davis, Melodie M., 1951-
  Whatever happened to dinner? : recipes and reflections for family mealtime / by Melodie M. Davis with Jodi Nisly Hertzler and Carmen Wyse.
    p. cm.
  ISBN 978-0-8361-9549-1 (pbk. : alk. paper)
  1. Cooking, American. 2. Dinners and dining—Social aspects. 3. Dinners and dining—Religious aspects. 4. Families. I. Hertzler, Jodi Nisly, 1973- II. Wyse, Carmen. III. Title.
  TX715.D2651163 2010
  641.5'4—dc22
                                              2010029447

WHATEVER HAPPENED TO DINNER?
Copyright © 2010 by Herald Press, Scottdale, PA 15683.
  Released simultaneously in Canada by Herald Press, Waterloo, Ont. N2L 6H7. All rights reserved
Library of Congress Control Number: 2010029447
International Standard Book Number: 978-0-8361-9549-1
Printed in United States of America
Cover by Reuben Graham

15 14 13 12 11 10   10 9 8 7 6 5 4 3 2 1

To order or request information please call 1-800-245-7894 or visit www.heraldpress.com.

To Jodi Nisly Hertzler and Carmen Wyse, recipe compilers and testers, and Sheri Hartzler, project coordinator. I wouldn't have tackled this without you.

Contents

Foreword

Some years ago my late colleague Alan Bloom wrote an academic best-seller, *The Closing of the American Mind*. I found one page in it with which to agree. As I recall, Professor Bloom was ruing the fact that religious illiteracy was rampant in America. Then he asked why this was so. The fault lay not with public schools, which were not free to teach and commend what religion taught about life. What had disappeared, said Bloom, was not "school" religion, but home-based religion. Jewish kids, he suggested, paid attention to stories about Moses just as Christian kids down the block did with Jesus stories. "We" had to and wanted to reckon with our parents, so we reckoned with these stories. They imparted them at dinner, where other important conversations about life took place. All that was disappearing, Bloom wrote, when fast-food stops replaced the family dinner table. Who discusses Jesus or virtue or deep things at drive-throughs?

We need to address Bloom's issue, but not in the same old way. "The same" usually comes with heavy doses of nostalgia, sentimentality, balloon-weight theories, boasting about how "we" once lived, and impractical practical advice. I am happy to say that Melodie Davis and company—poor souls Jodi and Carmen, who got to test recipes—have produced something different, and I am happy to commend it to you. Its many recipes are sandwiched among savory slices of story, theory, counsel, and biblical witness, all delivered deftly.

Who am I to commend this? My vita gives no clues as to why I should be credible. Historians, theologians, pastors, and journalists, among whom I thrive or throve, are not typed as experts on recipes and how-to advice about family living. Here are my credentials: first, I am a consumer, a regular at family dinner tables since 1955, and an inept preparer of food—though having been married and, as a widower, then married again. My late first wife, trained as a high-school teacher and de-trained as a mother, welcomed foster-, adoptive-, and foreign-student or inner-city drop-ins to our table. One year seven boys aged nine to fourteen gathered at our table nightly. We also described ourselves as "Victorian," since we had an almost hour-long reading circle each evening. Those of us who enjoyed that luxury can testify to the truth and usefulness of Ms. Davis's book.

The author knows how hard it is to act as she describes to enact the rites she implicitly prescribes. She knows that whatever the odds, including parents with complex schedules and children with ever more complex ones, much can be accomplished if a family seeks this better way with passion, and heroically works to arrange things.

I may be giving the wrong impression. This is not a crabby, bossy, know-it-all author's book. It comes across as a kind of friendly chat, salted with wisdom and peppered with helpful advice. Ordinarily when I edit or introduce a book with only a pre-publication set of loose pages in hand, I set them aside and wait for the book. This time I packed off some recipes to my wife, who serves visiting family and friends in addition to her hungry husband.

John Milton once famously described marriage as an "apt and cheerful conversation." He could have solidified the base of that description had he gone on to note that such conversation prospers best over a meal, graced by prayer and what Davis calls "reflections," such as one can find here. Enjoy.

—*Martin E. Marty*
Fairfax M. Cone Distinguished
Service Professor Emeritus
The University of Chicago

Preface

Foods and recipes are a personal thing. So personal that some great cooks don't believe in sharing recipes. Foods and recipes are also a family thing: what one family considers high eating and great comfort food, others wouldn't want to come near.

This inspirational cookbook is like a grand potluck meal, bringing together the efforts, cooks, and favorites of twelve families, all connected with the newly launched *Shaping Families* radio program in 2010. Along with the challenge of producing this program, the *Shaping Families* staff undertook the task of completing a cookbook pooling our collective efforts.

Whatever Happened to Dinner? began more than ten years ago, but it languished in files until Herald Press editors expressed an interest in seeing the proposal. Finding and testing recipes presented another huge hurdle, but having Jodi Nisly Hertzler and Carmen Wyse handle that part was a gift. They rounded out the selections in chapters where recipe contributions were thin or not varied, by adding some mouth-watering selections from their own kitchens.

What you get at this potluck is a wonderful variety of recipes you would never have gotten if they had just come from one family's recipe box and limited palette. Those who know the Davis family might page through this book and see recipes for couscous or quinoa and say, "Huh? I never thought of the Davises as a couscous or quinoa family. They are more of a fried-chicken-and-mashed-potato family." Jodi and Carmen's additions expanded and enriched the variety and viewpoints offered here.

This book is part cookbook; part reflection on the changing role of dinner in our culture; part celebration of family and community connections and how we can foster those connections through food, traditions, and sitting down together; part realistic acceptance of how things are in our busy world and practical handles for how to cope.

In each chapter, we'll also look at one biblical illustration, story, or parable that deals with some aspect of food, eating, or mealtime. This book will call families back together and to spiritual reflections even as it admits difficulties and heartaches. As families restrengthen their bonds and children are cherished, possibilities for communication increase, and ultimately we hope that all of us will cope just a little better with the realities that face us. Families can pull together even in the midst of a culture pulling us apart. We can flee the disconnectedness that threatens to undo us.

We hope you enjoy this collection of foods, memories, family stories, and most importantly, ideas on how you too can reclaim the somewhat diminishing family mealtime.

How the Recipes Came Together

Jodi and Carmen's job as food editors was to test the submitted recipes and select six per chapter, inserting their own ideas along the way. Seems simple, right? And in some ways, it was— their families needed to eat anyway. And there was a folder full of recipes to test, simplifying that all-too familiar conundrum *What am I cooking for supper tonight?*

But then they had to factor in the tastes of picky children, busy schedules, and their own ideas of what would make a good and helpful cookbook. It was trickier than first imagined to find the right variety of dishes for each chapter, balancing taste, nutrition, old family tried-and-trues, and personal inclinations toward in-season and whole foods.

So began a three-month odyssey of grocery shopping, cooking, recipe list construction and reconstruction, emails, phone calls, coffee meetings, trading leftovers, and the intermittent engagement of deaf ears to the complaints of children. Some recipes were major hits, but persuasion to eat unfamiliar foods sometimes had to be employed.

Mistakes were made, mishaps occurred, but through it all, there was an enjoyable feeling of community. Never before had the food editors regularly reported to a friend what they were cooking that night, followed by a detailed account of how the cooking process went and whether their families would eat the dish. Each of the cooks also had occasion to attempt foods they'd avoided in the past—cinnamon rolls (Jodi) and a cheeseball (Carmen)—and were pleasantly surprised more than once to find a new recipe that they could add to their own list of family favorites.

Along the way, they were reminded anew of the challenges families face simply trying to eat a meal together once a day—and neither cook works full time. Often a week would go by without having time to try a recipe, but then an afternoon would open up, and they'd make three or four new dishes for one meal—and invite company over to share.

As mothers of self-described "finicky" eaters (Carmen and Jodi have four boys and one girl between them), they strove to select recipes that would appeal to all members of the family and focused on simple, quick dishes that would ease the challenge of weeknight dinners. They steered away from processed foods whenever possible.

Feeding families is not a simple thing; it requires a lot of thought, planning, and energy. "But," Jodi and Carmen wrote after the project, "when it all turns out right—when we look across the table at children happily eating and talking about their day (it has happened once or twice)—it's definitely worth it. It's even worth it when they're kicking each other under the table and complaining about the "green stuff" in the rice—not in the moment, perhaps, but in the knowing that we're laying down a foundation of healthy eating habits and family togetherness."

If you try the recipes, let us know what you think on Facebook or this book's web page, www.mpn.net/dinner. We also hope you'll join the "Hang on to Dinner" Facebook group and share your efforts and experiences. You can also sign up to receive free weekly recipes along the lines of this book at the *Shaping Families* radio program website, ShapingFamilies.com. Get your kids to try the kid-friendly recipes, and share those successes and flops too. Also share your food and cultural background. These days we're not just trading recipes over the back fence (don't neglect that either) or calling Mom or Dad to find out how they made something, but everywhere we connect with each other. Growing, cooking, and sharing our own food is not just in, it's healthy, fun, cheaper, and something families have done for centuries.

—Melodie M. Davis, Singers Glen, Virginia
With food editors Jodi Nisly Hertzler and
Carmen Wyse, both of Harrisonburg, Virginia

Acknowledgments

I am very grateful to all those who contributed recipes for this collection beyond the numerous recipes from the food editors and some of my own favorites. Some of the speakers on the *Shaping Families* radio program sent contributions: Natalie Francisco, Rebecca Thatcher Murcia, and Emily Ralph, as did the program's website writer, Zachary Taylor. Third Way Media colleagues offering recipes included Burton Buller, Lowell and Betty Hertzler (Jodi's in-laws), Sheri Hartzler, Kimberly Metzler, and Lois Priest.

I am grateful also to the Herald Press team, who responded positively to the idea when it was suggested in a meeting: Ron Rempel, Russ Eanes, Amy Gingerich, and John Longhurst. And also to Byron Rempel-Burkholder and Reuben Graham, who served as editor and designer, respectively.

I would like to acknowledge my family, who have (mostly) enthusiastically endured my cooking all these years: my husband, Stuart; daughters, Michelle, Tanya and Doreen; and now son-in-law, Brian. The biggest complaint story they would tell was when

I tried to serve them mini tuna fish pizzas on hamburger buns, made with ketchup—they didn't taste nearly as good as when I had made them in a long-ago home economics class.

I also am grateful to the family I grew up in and my parents, Vernon and Bertha Miller, for my formative years on the farm and for how hard we all learned to work. I am grateful to my mother, who did almost all the cooking, and for her faithfulness in putting three delicious, comforting meals on the table every day, breakfast, dinner and supper, a feat I would learn to appreciate as a mother.

Finally, it was the readers of my syndicated Another Way newspaper column who first made me think this was a worthwhile topic after I wrote a column called "Whatever Happened to Dinner?" They responded enthusiastically, urging families to reclaim the family meal and sent along ideas, many of which you'll find in this book. And it was Mennonite Church USA graphic designer and friend Ken Gingerich who first observed, "That would make a good title for a book."

Introduction:
Whatever Happened to Dinner?

I felt like a visitor from another planet.

A few years back, I spoke in a high-school home-living class and asked the kids who did the cooking in their homes. The answers I got were: "It's every man for himself." "Everyone fixes what they want." "I pick up a sandwich every night. Fast food or whatever."

On one hand, I wanted to applaud their independence: these kids had seemingly achieved what I tried to teach my own kids—how to take care of themselves. On the other hand, I was aghast: Who is raising these kids? Whatever happened to dinner? At our Davis household, we usually had dinner together every night except Sunday, which we called "grab it and growl" night. What happens when the norm is "grab it and growl" and the family sits down together only for special occasions?

Whatever happened to the idea that even if you don't sit down together, someone makes some food, keeps it warm on the stove, and people try to make some stab at connecting with each other? What happens (I hate to think) to *nutritious* eating in the everyone-fixes-for-themselves scenario? One boy claimed to have been more or less taking care of himself before and after school since he was five years old, with an older brother occasionally looking in.

To use a business and academic cliché, there has been a paradigm shift from my home life to the current reality for many of today's kids. *Paradigm shift* is the hundred-dollar phrase we employ to simply say, "Things have changed."

I am of a generation when the family evening meal was a special time. I still operate from the ideal that even though Mom and Dad are working, families should have a gathered time at the end of the day with some kind of meal on the table. If Mom doesn't cook it, then Dad does or the children do. Sometimes it's pancakes and eggs for supper at our house. Other times it's a take-home pizza. On a good day it's fried chicken, mashed potatoes, gravy, and green beans. When our kids were teenagers learning to cook, they made spaghetti or tacos.

Many teens have jobs after school and extracurricular activities. According to the teacher who invited me to that high-school class, one of her students worked forty-five hours a week in addition to going to high school full time. When parents work a 3-11 shift or have to work overtime until 7 or 8 at night, a fifties-style meal with Dad at the head of the table carving roast beef isn't going to happen. With after-school sports and evening meetings, even a wild stab at having an actual supper together may be a stretch. But our family still tried. Why?

I think that eating together is one of the simple, basic structures of civilized life. Single people often hate having to eat alone. Unlike cats and dogs, who don't want you bothering them while they eat, most of us want companionship to be a part of our mealtimes. Sharing food, passing it, waiting on each other, talking about what happened at school or work helps us rise above the level of the dog or cat.

The answer is not to hearken back to the good old days that may have been more old than good. I do remember many fractured mealtimes as a family when I was growing up: Dad working late in the field; Mom growing frantic and pacing as she kept supper warm until 11:00 p.m. during long May planting days; staggered mealtimes because I or my sisters had basketball practice; Mom and Dad going away to a church or business banquet or meeting and we kids eating alone; meals when someone was sore at another member of the family and the only conversation was spoons and knives clinking angrily on plates.

But the norm, what we aimed for—the centering point for busy lives and schedules—was a meal together anytime between 4:45 and 7:00 p.m. And what I remember now about those mealtimes, even if they weren't all pleasant or perfect, was sitting around the kitchen table after a meal, telling stories and laughing. I remember making Chef Boyardee pizzas when Mom and Dad had to go to a banquet or dinner meeting. I recall the fun of packing a picnic supper of fried egg sandwiches to carry to Dad if he had to work really late in the field.

So even if you can't have a meal with your household every evening; even if it has to be eaten sometimes on the run; even if you have to pack an impromptu picnic and carry it to the office to eat with your accountant spouse during tax time—having some time gathered as a family is part of what family life is all about. If we raise our children without that glue, why bother to live in families at all? Why not each live in a doghouse or a pigpen?

I'm grateful for the work that the National Center on Addiction and Substance Abuse (CASA) at Columbia University has done on the importance of providing a nurturing environment for children. A 2009 CASA study found that, compared to teens who have frequent family dinners (five or more times per week), those who have infrequent family dinners (fewer than three per week) are twice as likely to use tobacco or marijuana, and twice as likely to expect to try drugs in the future.[1]

What are children getting when they sit down to a meal, besides the meat and potatoes—or salad and stir-fry? On a good day at a family meal, children of any age get attention that leads to parents and kids who are more involved with each other's lives. Children get useful practice in the art of dinner conversation (we hope). They get times of laughter and downright silliness; I remember especially how we three girls would collapse in laughter sometimes to the point of tears. It can be a precious family bonding time.

Dinner may also be the only time the family gathers to pray and ask a blessing. Somehow that simple daily act—especially if you've been arguing or grouchy right before—forces families to change gears and perhaps find peace amid the daily troubles.

These intangible gifts go a long way toward giving kids the glue they need to grow up with the ability to navigate the negative pressures they face in our society.

The loss of family dinnertime is one of the more unfortunate losses of our age—and we can probably blame it on good old Henry Ford and his invention: the automobile. It has helped all of us be more mobile and less likely to stay home. During the 1990s and the decade after that, U.S. workers were clocking more hours on the job than any other industrialized country. At that time, almost one-third of workers regularly clocked more than the standard forty-hour week. One-fifth worked more than fifty hours.[2]

In contrast to past times, when many worked out of or near their homes in cottage industries or farms, the car and mass transit have enabled most of us to work an average of 24.3 minutes away (driving). In the United States, if the average vacation from work is two weeks, Americans spend more time commuting than they do on vacation; the average commuting time is more than 100 hours a year—*if* you're lucky. Many commute an hour or more a *day*.[3]

As I have watched these numbers and written on this topic in my newspaper column during the last ten years, there has been a slight increase in the number of families eating together, especially during the last two years of the global recession (2008–2010). In 2009, 59 percent of youth in the CASA study reported having dinner with their families at least five times a week. Parents report a similar count, with 62 percent of parents saying they have frequent family dinners.[4] These trends might be a sign of hope that families are getting the message regarding the importance of family mealtime. But it could also be an anomaly due to the recession: when one or both parents are out of work and at home, they may be able to cook more. Could we speculate, then, that our affluence is one of the factors that has contributed to long-term mealtime trends of the last forty years?

Longer working hours and commutes are only part of the problem. Overscheduled kids are another huge part. Between soccer practice, ballet lessons, swimming, and piano, family dinners get short shrift. And once kids turn fifteen or sixteen, many also hold down part-time jobs, cutting further into family mealtime. Also, about two-thirds (64 percent) of all families with children between eight and eighteen have the television set on during meals.[5] Studies also track distractions like texting and status updates on social media during mealtimes. These don't help family conversation either.

As we talk about the loss of family dinnertime, it is appropriate to ask, when did it ever become a tradition to begin with? And how can we recover such a valuable gathering time, given today's family schedules? We'll explore these questions more in the rest of this book.

● ● ● ● ● ● ● ● ● ●

Probably the most famous meal in the Bible was the one shared by Jesus with his disciples right before his arrest and crucifixion. We call it the Last Supper, and Christians reenact it as often as once a day in some traditions, once a week, once a month, or once or twice a year. Many famous paintings depict it.

Jesus' last meal with his friends was a ritual meal: the Jewish Passover commemorating the children of Israel's miraculous escape from Egypt in the time of Moses (see Exodus 12). If ever there was a meal on the run, it was that meal, with people fleeing not only for their own lives, but also for the freedom of their whole nation. Verse 11 describes the directions given them: "This is how you are to eat it: with your cloak tucked into your belt, your sandals on your feet and your [car keys] in your hand. Eat it in haste; it is the LORD's Passover."

The meal and food instructions in Exodus 12 make a fascinating study—especially the notes about the Israelites carrying out large kneading troughs of unleavened bread dough wrapped in cloth because "they did not have time to prepare food for themselves." That image reminds me of one of the *Shaping Families* radio speakers, Rebecca Thatcher Murcia, who told about a time she had neglected to make anything for the Easter potluck brunch at her church. She simply carried cinnamon roll dough with her to church and sneaked into the kitchen between church and Sunday school to assemble and cook her rolls. Because of her neglect, worshippers got a special treat that day: fresh, hot cinnamon rolls right out of the oven (see chapter 5 for the recipe). Many of us would have just picked up something from a grocery store on the way to church, but Rebecca had a creative response to the "no time, got kids" excuse of every parent. Her rolls were truly Passover rolls in the best Exodus tradition. Exodus 12 reminds us that, while keeping family mealtime is an important goal, we have a lot of company when schedules and priorities are hectic—company that goes clear back to the earliest days of civilization.

● ● ● ● ● ● ● ● ● ●

After I posted a note on Facebook about this book, a mother and elementary school teacher from my church, Lauren, asked me more about it. Her sons are ages thirteen and ten, and she was immediately drawn to the topic. "We have worked very hard, even when it isn't easy, to have dinner together most nights," she said. "It is just something I feel is important." We discussed the studies and statistics that show how eating together helps to work against kids' involvement in drugs, gangs, crime, and the like—though there is no guarantee of such an outcome. "Yeah, I've heard about those," she said. "I'm not sure why it would work, but it seems like keeping dinner is worth the effort."

Studies—mostly coming from CASA—show that kids who don't have frequent family dinners were likelier to be able to get their hands on marijuana within one hour and to have friends who use marijuana or Ecstasy.

Maybe even more important, says Elizabeth Planet, CASA's vice president, "teens who have frequent family dinners are likelier to get A's and B's in school and have excellent relationships with their parents. Having dinner as a family is one of the easiest ways to create routine opportunities for parental engagement and communication."[6] A National Merit Scholarship study of their award winners discovered that the one thing that linked the winners was that their families had dinner together.[7]

No one expects that such families are "better" or perfect. Lauren went on to share with me how, to keep her boys from endless bickering at breakfast, they agreed on a routine in which one son gets the kitchen (and the television in the kitchen) for twenty minutes in the morning while the other showers and gets ready for school, and then the other son gets the space for twenty minutes—their way of keeping peace in the household.

CASA's founder and chairman Joseph A. Califano Jr., the former U.S. Secretary of Health, Education and Welfare, says, "Of course there are no silver bullets; teen substance abuse can strike any family."[8] I would add that many teens struggling with depression or another mental illness also unfortunately get into alcohol and drugs as a way to self-medicate, which is different from trying drugs just for something different or to be cool or for recreation. I know families who had dinner together practically every night yet have young adults with habits that are excruciatingly difficult to kick. To them, this kind of advice probably sounds shallow or hollow. The family dinner, therefore, is not a recipe for avoiding drugs, but it can be one way to increase the odds that kids won't turn to drugs for those feelings of love, self-worth, and acceptance.

Califano goes on: "With everyone living such busy lives these days, the family dinner becomes an important tool to raising drug-free children because gathering around the table as a family shows kids just how much their parents care about them and sends a message that their parents are there for them."[9] His 2009 book, *How to Raise a Drug-Free Kid: The Straight Dope for Parents*, includes a chapter on the importance of family dinners.

Back to my conversation with Lauren. That same Sunday morning, her oldest son and the entire youth group were leading worship focusing on the "fruit of the Spirit": love, joy, peace, patience, kindness, goodness, faithfulness, gentleness, and self-control (Galatians 5:22). They made up several skits, and at one point, all the youth were to give one-line definitions of *love*. Her son Andrew's statement was a perfect capstone to our preservice conversation: "Love is my mom making dinner."

Making dinner: a way to show love and to experience it as a family. I can't think of a better way to summarize what this book is about.

• • • • • • • • •

Michelle's Chicken Casserole

Melodie Davis

This is an easy recipe from my oldest daughter, Michelle, who liked recipes with exact proportions as she was learning to cook. She was frustrated with my instructions to put in a little of this or that, so she was happy to get this very specific and simple recipe from a friend. Similar to other recipes of this type, it makes an easy one-dish meal. Substitute cooked and cubed chicken tenders or any leftover chicken.

1 10-ounce / 300 g package frozen, chopped broccoli
1 can (10¾ oz.) / 330 g condensed cream of broccoli soup
1 large can (9¾ oz.) / 300 g white chicken, drained
2 cups / 500 ml cheddar cheese, shredded

Preheat oven to 350° F / 180° C. Cook broccoli according to package directions, in a pan or in the microwave. Drain. Put the broccoli in the bottom of an ungreased 9x13-inch baking dish. Add soup and chicken, and top with cheese. Bake for 30 minutes, until bubbly. Makes 4–6 servings.

Suggestion: This recipe makes an excellent topping for baked potatoes.

Broccoli Noodle Soup with Italian Sausage

Carmen Wyse

1 pound / 500 g Italian sausage links, cut in ½-inch pieces
8 cups (2 boxes) / 2 L chicken stock
1 cup / 250 ml water
½ pound / 250 g noodles, any shape
4 cups / 1 L frozen broccoli

Brown the sausage in a large soup pot. Add the chicken stock and water. Cover and let simmer 10 or more minutes. Add the noodles and cook for another 5 minutes. Add the broccoli, cover until the soup comes to a simmer, and cook an additional 5 minutes, or until the broccoli is tender and the noodles are cooked. Makes 4–6 servings.

Pasta & Broccoli Alfredo

Jodi Nisly Hertzler

I found a variation of this recipe on the Internet when I was newly married and not very experienced in the kitchen. I was looking for lower-fat versions of some of our favorite foods. This is one of the few recipes from that kitchen-disaster-prone period of my life that has endured. It's quick, simple—and my whole family likes it. Freshly grated Parmesan cheese really adds something to this dish, but if you're in a hurry, the bagged kind works too.

1 pound / 500 g pasta (we prefer thin spaghetti)
1 pound / 500 g broccoli florets (thawed, if using frozen)
1 12-ounce / 340 g can nonfat evaporated milk
2 tablespoons flour
1½ cup / 375 ml shredded Parmesan cheese

Cook pasta according to directions, adding broccoli during the last 5 minutes. Cook until tender. Drain.

While pasta cooks, blend evaporated milk and flour over low heat, whisking frequently until hot (don't boil—you want it just warm enough to melt the cheese). Whisk in the cheese gradually, melting each handful before adding the next. As soon as all the cheese is melted, pour over pasta and broccoli, toss well, and serve. Makes 6 servings.

Tanya's Mix

Melodie Davis

This evolved out of my second daughter Tanya's experiences at camp, cooking "tin foil" dinners over the open fire. This adaptation can include whatever vegetables the kids want, such as chopped cabbage or carrots, for what is essentially a stove-top casserole. Quantities can also be adjusted according to whether it is for one person or six. This is a great recipe for using up leftover green beans or corn from your fridge or freezer.

1 pound / 500 g hamburger meat
2–3 medium potatoes, peeled and cubed
1 15- or 16-ounce can / 500 ml green beans, or approximately
      1 pint / 500 ml
½ can corn (or approximately 1 cup / 250 ml frozen corn)
½ teaspoon salt
Pepper to taste

Fry hamburger in skillet. When most of it is turning brown, add cubed potatoes. When hamburger is cooked through, drain extra grease. Add seasoning. Keep stirring hamburger and potatoes while potatoes cook. When potatoes are almost soft (10–15 minutes), chop beans into small pieces and add them. Add corn. Cook all together 5–7 minutes.

Note: to speed cooking time, consider microwaving potatoes a minute or two before cubing.

Quesadilla Pie

Jodi Nisly Hertzler

Quesadillas have long been one of my go-to ideas for something quick and easy that kids enjoy eating. This recipe simplifies things even more, and in one pie plate creates a tasty one-dish meal that the whole family likes. It can be customized to your family's preferences and the contents of your pantry and garden. Kids enjoy choosing toppings to put on each layer.

4 large flour tortillas (9 inches / 23 cm diameter)
Butter, softened
½ pound / 250 g grated cheese (mild or sharp cheddar, or
        Monterey Jack)

Filling Options:
- Beans (refried beans, black beans, pinto beans)
- Tomatoes, chopped and drained
- Onions, diced (consider scallions or red onions)
- Cooked chicken, pork, or beef (chopped or shredded)
- Corn
- Summer squash, chopped
- Mushrooms, chopped
- Peppers, diced (bell peppers of any color, chilies, jalapenos)
- Olives, sliced or chopped
- Salsa
- Cumin and/or chili powder (sprinkle lightly over beans or meat for extra flavor)

Garnishes:
- Chopped avocado or guacamole
- Chopped cilantro
- Sour cream

- Salsa
- Shredded iceberg lettuce dressed with vinegar and salt

Preheat oven to 350° F / 180° C. Butter the bottom and sides of a 10-inch pie dish.

Place one tortilla on the bottom of the dish. Sprinkle shredded cheese over the tortilla. Add your chosen filling ingredients and layer the tortillas. Add 3 layers of fillings, mixing and matching the above options in any way, with a generous sprinkling of cheese. Top layers with a tortilla, and spread butter over its surface.

Cover with aluminum foil. Put in the oven for 30 minutes. Remove the foil and increase the heat to 400° F / 200° C. Cook for another 15–20 minutes, until the top is lightly browned and the cheese is bubbly. Remove from oven and let cool 10 minutes before serving. Top with garnishes of your choice.

Makes 4–6 servings.

1

• • • • • • • • • •

Even Cave Kids Knew What Dinner Was

I want to dig into history a little. If we think gathering as a family for mealtime is so important, where do we get this idea? From fifties television shows? Our memories of earlier eras? How far back does mealtime go? Did cave kids know what dinner was? What does history and archaeology show?

We'll look at just a few snippets of food history to get a sense of how mealtime has evolved: others have gone into much more detail, including Martha Visser in her delightfully titled work *Much Depends on Dinner: The Extraordinary History and Mythology, Allure and Obsessions, Perils and Taboos of an Ordinary Meal* (Grove Press, 1999).

The earliest peoples were "gatherers" of whatever they could find—and maybe ate on the run. At first they ate fruits, mushrooms, nuts, roots, and seeds, and eventually they learned to hunt for meat. Before humans learned how to make fire, they probably roasted some meats over fires that started in nature. But once they learned how to make pots for boiling and cooking stews,[1] their menus began to expand. As some of these early discoveries were made, gathering around a fire at the end of the day or at the conclusion of a hunt was standard practice, indicating that eating together has long been a foundational social experience among humans.

Moving forward in time, research of Pacific Northwest coastal peoples from about two thousand years ago reveals that they probably ate two meals a day.[2] Having access to bountiful catches from the ocean meant they had to do less hunting and gathering than those in other locations. The first meal was served around ten in the morning, after the morning work. The next meal was served around sundown. The men would sit down first, on a mat. Before coming to the low table, they had to wash their hands and face, twice. They dried themselves with softened cedar bark that acted as towels. They would also take a long drink from the drinking bucket. It was not considered good manners to drink at the table.

Courses were served on wooden platters. These platters were about a foot and half long and were ornately carved from cedar. Places were hollowed out to hold various foods. There was even a hollowed-out spot to hold fish oil, for food dunking. They used spoons to eat, carved from bone or shell.

Once the men were served, the women would join them on the mats. The family talked to each other during meals. It was a social time, a time to relax before returning to work. They often invited people from outside their family to meals.

The concept of family itself is interesting to look at through the ages. One place we can get information is the Bible. In Genesis, all members of a household were included in the designation of "family," including concubines (live-in mistresses), servants, slaves, visitors, and prisoners of war if necessary. There was polygamy, and that made the family unit even more complicated.

Family could also refer to the entire clan or tribe. So a household could literally encompass an entire nation. In Ezra 8, some families returning from exile in Babylon had several hundred members. Members of a clan accepted communal responsibility for other members, including assistance in time of need, protection, sharing work, loyalty.

Sacrifices in the temple in the Old Testament were actually meals—carefully prescribed and ritualistic. The manna meals sent by God in the wilderness suggest that mealtime was morning and evening. In Exodus 16 we read that the children of Israel had quail to eat in the evening and manna in the morning.

Research shows that ordinary Romans in the time just prior to Christ dined simply. Meals were prepared by the mother or by female slaves under her direction. A table was set up in the atrium of the house. The father, mother, and children sat on stools around the table. Often the kids waited on their parents. Table knives and forks were unknown, but the Romans had spoons like ours today. Food was cut into finger food before serving, and eaten using fingers or a spoon. In the last two centuries of the Roman Empire, this simple style of living changed a bit. A separate dining room was designed. In place of benches or stools, there were dining couches.

Upper-class Romans had dinners that were quite elaborate. The men had the dinner parties; rules of decency required that women and children ate separately. They ate many different foods, drank lots of wine, and spent hours at dinner. Often the men's dinner parties had entertainment, such as dancing girls or a play, or both. Men reclined on couches arranged around the dinner table. In their separate dining quarters, women and children usually sat on chairs. As things loosened up in the later years of the empire, decent women could go to a dinner party.[3]

As families became smaller, as they certainly were by New Testament times, and as people began to define family as a mother, father, and children, there was less feeling of responsibility for others. That is why, perhaps, we see reminders in the New Testament concerning obligations toward widows and orphans. The upside was that feuds between families also diminished as this sense of communal responsibility lessened.

We can guess that meals were important for the family in Bible times. In the previous chapter we saw how Jesus drew his disciples together one last time for a meal together. The Passover meal functioned as a meal of remembrance with religious significance, but it was nevertheless an important "family" time together.

In the movie version of the Broadway musical *Fiddler on the Roof*, set in Russia prior to World War II, one of the most moving and vivid scenes is the family participating in a Passover meal. Family members scurry to make it to the table by sundown. Who says earlier generations really had more time or were less stressed? The mother—plain, down-to-earth Golde—reigns like a bride with partial veil at the meal, even in that patriarchal system. Children ask the ritual questions. The mundane and even impoverished home takes on an atmosphere of a beautiful, earthy, still-life painting. The profane, ordinary food is transformed into sacred fare. The routine of eating is transformed into holy communion with God.

All cultures and societies have rituals or celebrations involving food or feast days: weddings, funerals, birthdays, coronations. We will indeed have lost something precious, ancient, and "civilized" if we lose the art of having a decent meal together. Food gives us life, and mealtime gives one form of community.

James Krabill, Mennonite Mission Network vice president for Global Ministries, points out that "in stark contrast to the North American pattern, most people living elsewhere in the world devote considerable time and energy to meal-making and taking. And they rarely do it alone, in isolation from others." He quotes Kenyan priest and anthropologist John Mutiso-Mbinda, saying that in the African context "a meal is always a communal affair." "Eating together is a sign of being accepted to share life and equality."[4]

Someone has pointed out that meals prepared and served to a group of people or family take on a certain ritual quality: food is prepared, the table is set, people are called to the table, grace or prayers are said, the food is passed. Rituals like this bring people together in common, routine experiences that can be a calming balm after a busy day. Eating food together is a bonding experience that can ease tension, make conversation go easier, make strangers less self-conscious. Mealtime may be one of the oldest rituals known to humans.

In contrast, the automobile, which has been around only one hundred years and launched our mobile society, brought about the growth of restaurants and fast-food chains and prepared, packaged foods. The car has led to more and more people just grabbing dinner on the run.

Our modern industrial and information ages, as opposed to agricultural times when people stopped working at sundown, mean families have members working at all hours of the day and night. There is no time for dinner.

And who says cave kids were uncivilized? Maybe it is *our* kids who are uncivilized, eating from a box, with their hands, shoveling food into their mouths in front of the television. Or maybe we parents are too.

● ● ● ● ● ● ● ● ● ●

Bread is a staple from ancient times and from around the world, in all its different forms: from manna to pita to nan to tortilla to rye loaves to heavy German black bread. It is often the "staff of life" for fledging eaters.

When I was a child, like many children I didn't have wide-ranging tastes, so I focused on bread. I remember going to homes of people who had worked in overseas settings, and they frequently served exotic dishes that were definitely different from my Mennonite mother's plain meat-and-potatoes-and-beans-corn-or-peas cooking. So I would always look for the bread, whatever it was, and fill up on that after trying the requisite three bites. I never starved, and I later learned to fully enjoy foods from around the world. So don't worry if you have young ones who fill up on bread, as long as they at least try new foods. It takes time for a tongue to learn to like certain foods.

Bread is a staple in the Bible, too, and allusions to yeast are frequent. As Jesus spoke in parables, which were stories that often contained hidden messages that his enemies would have trouble deciphering or using to condemn him, one of his simple parables was no more than a "tweet": "The kingdom of heaven is like yeast that a woman took and mixed into a large amount of flour until it worked all through the dough" (Matthew 13:33). That's it. That's the whole parable. The kingdom of heaven, or God's reign, has good yeast spread throughout that affects every spore or aspect of our lives. Once unloosed, the yeast affects the whole mass of bread dough, raising it into something good and life giving and oh so tasty.

In the wrong environment, of course, yeast can lose its power. It is the same with followers of Jesus. Ideally, the yeast of the kingdom of heaven gets spread throughout our lives, and as our lives touch others, we spread that good and wholesome message.

My late father-in-law, Hershal Davis, would frequently begin a meal with us by saying after the blessing, "Take bread and eat." It was his way of saying "dig in." I still love that simple blessing, which emphasizes the universality of a basic piece of bread.

As you enjoy bread in its different forms, think about how it joins you with ancient peoples and across cultures. Remember also the yeast of God's kingdom, and help it spread to those around you.

● ● ● ● ● ● ● ● ● ● ●

Doreen's Oatmeal Bread

Melodie Davis

This comes "more or less" from More-with-Less Cookbook, *the classic Mennonite cookbook that came out the year my husband and I were married. My copy is missing its cover and spattered with oil and flour. In our version, we use a little more flour than that recipe called for, and we always use two packages of yeast rather than one.*

Combine in large bowl:
1 cup / 250 ml quick oats
½ cup / 125 ml whole wheat flour
½ cup / 125 ml brown sugar
1 tablespoon salt
2 tablespoons butter or margarine

Pour 2 cups / 500 ml boiling water over mixture in bowl.

Separately dissolve:

2 packages dry yeast in

½ cup / 125 ml warm water

When batter is cooled to lukewarm, add the yeast mixture. Stir in 5½ cups / 1.4 L white flour (you'll probably add another ½ cup / 125 ml in kneading). When dough is stiff, turn onto a floured board and knead 5–10 minutes. Place in greased bowl, cover, and let rise until doubled. Punch down and let rise again. Shape into 2 loaves and place in greased 9x5x3-inch pans. Bake at 350° F / 180° C for 25–30 minutes. Cool on rack. Brush loaves with butter or margarine for a soft crust.

Suggestions: For a little added nutrition, substitute some or all whole wheat flour for the white flour. If you substitute more than half, the bread will have a denser texture, and you may need less flour, but the result is still tasty.

Whole Wheat Rolls

Burton Buller

When Aunt Jean's turn came to host family feasts, we kids looked forward to the whole wheat buns she would always serve. They were so light, so soft, and so delicious. Only much later did I discover they were made with cottage cheese. Had I known that then, I likely would not have even tried them, and I would have denied myself a treat. Now they are fun to make and serve. And when I'm adding the cottage cheese, Aunt Jean always comes to mind, bringing memories of wonderful Thanksgivings around her large table.

2 cups / 500 ml whole wheat flour
1½ cup / 375 ml white flour
2 packages yeast
½ teaspoon soda
1½ cup / 375 ml cream-style (4% milk fat) cottage cheese
¼ cup / 50 ml brown sugar
½ cup / 125 ml margarine or butter
1 tablespoon salt
2 eggs
½ cup / 125 ml water

Stir together 2 cups / 500 ml whole wheat flour, yeast, and soda in the bowl of a heavy-duty mixer. Set aside.

Heat cottage cheese, water, sugar, margarine or butter, and salt until warm. Stir to melt the butter or margarine. Add to dry mixture, and mix until combined. Add eggs. Beat with a dough hook (a paddle attachment works too) at low-medium speed. Gradually add remaining wheat flour and all white flour to make a moderately stiff dough (you may need to let the mixer run for a while, until the dough is no longer sticky).

Turn dough onto a floured surface and knead a minute or two until smooth and elastic. Place dough in a greased bowl, turning once. Cover and let rise until double in size. Shape into 24 balls (flatten to shape into buns). Let rise until double again.

Bake at 350° F / 180° C for 12–15 minutes, until golden brown.

Suggestions: These make excellent hamburger or sandwich buns, soft and light. Consider serving them with the Bean Burgers (recipe in chapter 6) or the Parmesan Chicken Burgers (chapter 3).

Morning Glory Muffins

Burton Buller

1 cup / 250 ml grated carrots
⅓ cup / 75 ml grated apple
¼ cup / 50 ml raisins
¼ cup / 50 ml walnuts
¼ cup / 50 ml coconut
1 teaspoon cinnamon
1 egg
⅓ cup / 75 ml canola oil
1 teaspoon vanilla
2 cups / 500 ml flour
½ cup / 125 ml sugar
1 teaspoon soda
¼ teaspoon salt

Preheat oven to 350° F / 180° C. Combine all ingredients, and mix. Spoon batter into muffin pans. Bake for 20 minutes. Makes 1 dozen.

Suggestions: For a healthier version, substitute unsweetened applesauce for the oil, and replace up to half the flour with whole wheat.

Tortillas

Carmen Wyse

On one camping trip, I tried making breakfast tacos out of store-bought tortillas. They were crumbly and weren't working well. A camping companion said she always makes her own tortillas. I figured if she could, I could too, and I have been making them ever since. I usually make a double batch and keep the leftovers for snacks throughout the week. I can always count on a big hug from my twelve-year-old son when he sees me starting to make these.

3 cups / 750 ml flour (I use up to 1 cup whole wheat)
1 teaspoon salt
½–1 teaspoon baking powder
⅓ cup / 75 ml vegetable oil
1 cup / 250 ml warm water

Mix the dry ingredients together. Add the vegetable oil, and mix with pastry cutter or forks until crumbly like cornmeal. Add 1 cup warm water. Knead a bit to bring it together, cover with plastic wrap, and let it sit for 30 minutes to several hours. Form into 12 balls.

Heat a cast-iron (or whatever you have) skillet to medium high. Roll each tortilla out as thin as you can, and plop it in the hot skillet. When it starts blistering, turn it over for about 30 seconds. Sometimes I hold the edges down some to keep the tortilla from puffing up. Put it in a tortilla warmer or under several kitchen towels.

Cornmeal Whole Wheat Waffles

Jodi Nisly Hertzler

These may be the tastiest waffles I've ever made, and I love the fact that they use whole grains. This is also an easy recipe that you mix the night before. In the morning, all you have to do is whip out the waffle iron, and in minutes, everyone in the family is happy. Freeze leftovers (but put a paper towel or napkin between them so they don't stick together), and pop them in the toaster for an easy school-day breakfast.

2 eggs, beaten
2 cups / 500 ml milk (or substitute half or all buttermilk)
⅔ cup / 150 ml yellow cornmeal
1⅓ cup / 325 ml whole wheat flour
2¼ teaspoons yeast
1 teaspoon sugar
1½ teaspoons salt
1 stick butter, melted and cooled a little
¼ teaspoon baking soda

In a mixing bowl, whisk together the eggs and milk. Add the flour, cornmeal, yeast, sugar, and salt. Stir in the melted butter.

Cover the bowl and refrigerate overnight (or make them in the morning and serve them for supper).

When ready to serve, heat up the waffle iron. Add the baking soda, and whisk well. (The batter is runnier than most recipes I've used, and doesn't rise as much in the waffle iron, resulting in waffles that are less bready and more on the crispy side.) Cook according to your waffle iron's instructions.

Cranberry Orange Bread

Carmen Wyse

I asked a coworker for this recipe after she brought it to a work potluck. It is moist and tasty.

½ package fresh cranberries, chopped
½ cup / 125 ml chopped nuts (optional)
1 tablespoon orange zest
1 cup / 250 ml flour
1 cup / 250 ml 100% bran cereal
1 cup / 250 ml sugar
1½ teaspoon baking powder
1 teaspoon salt
½ teaspoon soda
2 tablespoons butter
¾ cup / 175 ml orange juice
1 egg, beaten

Preheat oven to 350° F / 180° C. Grease and flour 1 loaf pan.

Mix cereal and orange juice, and let stand 5 minutes.

Mix flour, sugar, baking powder, salt, and soda. Make a well in the dry ingredients. Melt butter and add along with orange juice mixture, egg, and orange zest. Stir just to moisten. Fold in cranberries and nuts. Spoon into prepared loaf pan and bake 1 hour or until a toothpick comes out clean. Cool 15 minutes and then remove from pan. Cool completely.

Quick Honey Wheat Bread

Jodi Nisly Hertzler

This is an excellent finishing touch to a soup meal. Five minutes of work, an hour in the oven while you get the rest of your meal together, and you have warm, fresh bread ready for the table.

2 cups / 500 ml wheat flour
1 cup / 250 ml white flour
1 teaspoon salt
1 teaspoon baking soda
1⅔ cup / 400 ml buttermilk or plain yogurt
½ cup / 125 ml honey
1 egg

Preheat oven to 325° F / 160° C. Grease an 8x4- or 9x5-inch loaf pan.

Mix the dry ingredients together. In a separate bowl, mix the wet ingredients. Stir the liquid into the dry ingredients, then pour into the loaf pan.

Bake about an hour, until the loaf is firm and a toothpick inserted into the center comes out clean. Cool on a rack for 15 minutes before removing from the pan. Can be served warm or room temperature.

2

• • • • • • • • •

The Family That Gardens Together Eats Together

I stepped into the old barn that held so many wonderful memories from my childhood. "Ugh," said my children with their citified noses. "It smells."

It was their first trip to my childhood home, when they were ages five through ten. To me the smells were part of the ambiance: the cobwebs, the ancient beams, the hay piled in the mow.

The soil is in my veins, I'm happy to say. I was lucky enough to grow up on a 128-acre spread in northern Indiana, but I didn't know how fortunate. All I knew then was that it was work: gathering eggs; driving a tractor to cultivate corn in the fields (I couldn't plow or plant good enough to be trusted with those more tricky operations); helping make hay or straw; working a large garden, an orchard, and a large patch where we grew watermelon and cantaloupe.

"I used to know every inch of this land," I told my girls. "The creeks at both ends of the farm, the woods, these trees . . . " and I looked up, stunned at the lovely tall oak at the edge of the yard. The oak I remembered was no more than fifteen feet tall, planted by my father. A thickness grabbed at my throat.

How wonderful to walk this land again, I thought, grateful to the large Amish family that now lives there for permission to do so. They gladly said we could walk where we wished, almost like they were aware that God owns all land anyway and people are only temporary caretakers.

"This is such wonderful land," the father told us. "A good variety of soils, from light sand to heavy muck. We like it here so much."

I was happy to hear that. We want people to be happy in the homes we have loved. The Amish farmer's words about God's gift of good soil reminds me of the parable of the soil found in Matthew 13:3-9. In my Bible it is called the parable of the sower, but I've always thought this parable was really about the dirt—the soil. And indeed it is at one level; it explains how, when a farmer sows his seeds, some fall on the path, where birds quickly eat them up; some fall in rocky ground, where they can't send down roots and soon die; some seeds land among thorns, which thwarts their growth. The seeds that fall on good soil bring a good harvest in varying yields. We usually interpret this to mean that you should expect that when you sow the seeds of the good news about Jesus, you have similar results. Another interpretation focuses on people as the soil: what kind of environment do you offer to the gospel message? Rocky? Weedy? Fertile?

In *Parables for Today*, author Alyce McKenzie points out that the yield described in this parable of "100 times" what was sown is actually "too good to be true."[1] That would have been a miraculous, almost impossible yield. So God is saying that all yields from our efforts at sowing seed are due to the miraculous grace of God—true whether you are planting literal seeds in the ground or witnessing to God's goodness.

Whatever your interpretation, my point here is that raising some food in soil should be a basic experience of every child. They should learn in a hands-on way where their food comes from—not the store, not Mom and Dad, not the fast-food window, but from God, the sower. We tend to value things we understand, and knowing more about food production can help families bond around their meals.

I need to eat more mindfully myself. As I write this, I'm enjoying a simple breakfast of Italian bread, butter, peach jam, and coffee. I need to take the time to dissect the origins of my good food, all dependent on soil, water, air, and sunshine: the flour stemming from wheat; the butter coming from cows who feed on grass and corn; the peach from a tree that has been carefully grown and nurtured for many years; the coffee beans raised on a bush on some South American ranch; the water from my own well many feet below my patch of land. How seldom do I stop to truly appreciate the many hands who've given me what I consume all day long. I need to make sure I teach these things to my children as well.

● ● ● ● ● ● ● ● ● ●

Part of my family's old Indiana farm has gone the way of good farms everywhere—broken up into smaller plots for attractive lawns and homes. Still, there's lots of land left for farming if you look. Traveling through Pennsylvania, Ohio, and Indiana, I'm struck by the wide, beautiful farms stretching out on both sides of the highways. Living in the eastern United States, one gets used to seeing small, cramped pieces of land being used for farms: little strips of terraced crops on hillsides, larger fields in fertile valleys. Further west, we are always in awe of the vast fields of Kansas, Iowa, Nebraska, or Manitoba: people still farm huge plots of land!

Small family farms have long been an endangered species. I remember my first awakening to the fact that farming—my idyllic upbringing—was changing. From northern Indiana we moved to northern Florida and observed the trend toward corporations owning vast stretches of farmland. Dad would talk about how the corporations, unlike him, didn't care if they lost money on their endeavors, because it was a tax write-off.

Writing in *Sojourners* magazine more than a decade ago, Judith Bortner Heffernan, executive director of a network of United Methodist churches focused on rural America, wrote that in "just one or two generations, the [North American] decentralized family farm system, the envy of the rest of the world as a highly efficient producer of abundant food and fiber, has increasingly become a centralized, corporate-controlled, factory food system. While farm families struggle to survive on an average of three to four percent return on their investment, the food firms expect to receive at least 20 percent."[2]

Heffernan was at the cutting edge then in pointing out the need to support more localized and personalized food systems, revealing that on average, the food we consume travels about 1,800 miles to our plates. She encouraged supporting local farmers' markets and cooperatives, and stores and restaurants that buy from local, independent producers.

Two church friends in Virginia, Nancy and Harvey, helped to make me more aware of things that were so much a part of my "fishbowl" growing up on a farm that I didn't even recognize them. Harv and Nancy owned a one-acre "farmette" in a village constructed in the old style: a town square with surrounding acres squared off into farming plots. They baked bread and raised plants, flowers, and vegetables for the local farmers market and also kept sheep and chickens. They were neighbors and fellow church members, so while our children were growing up, we frequently took care of their animals when they needed to go away.

The kids and I loved those experiences of gathering the eggs, feeding the sheep, and making sure all the livestock had water. We didn't enjoy it so much in the winter, when we were reminded of how difficult farming is: breaking up the frozen water for the sheep, getting clothes and hands frozen from broken water pipes or hoses, wrestling a chubby, stubborn sheep out of the part of the barn where the feed was kept. Nancy, the CEO of a local complex providing care for those with physical and mental limitations, would wax philosophical about the difficulties, saying that the farm kept her aware of the cycles of nature.

When we work in a factory, office, school, or hospital, we can go weeks and months in indoor environments, never even aware that animals' drinking water outside is freezing or that early shoots of roadside asparagus and backyard dandelion can provide food and fresh nutrition in earliest spring. People in agrarian cultures are certainly more aware of these cycles of nature and their dependence on God's hand for all they have.

The possibility exists that unless we take steps to change the tide, people will someday have little or no recollection of where food comes from or of sitting down to a family meal together. I doubt we'll consume our nutrition only through a handful of pills or IV ports, but I don't have as much trouble imagining that people will view eating as a solitary, independent endeavor in which they fix or buy what they want or need and worry about no one else. They will eat without even being mindful of the marvelous gift of food.

• • • • • • • • • •

Gardening can help us remember our dependence on God. Even if it is only a tomato plant on the patio or deck, it can make us appreciate the time and care needed to nurse its fruit to completion. Buying from local farmers is one way that almost everyone can preserve a bit of the gardening or agrarian lifestyle. Gardening practices can help us come to appreciate our reliance on God, nature, and other humans who grow our food. We teach our children rich knowledge they frequently do not gain in a textbook or classroom. We give them and ourselves fresher, healthier food that is infinitely better tasting. They learn the value of hard work and experience the disappointment and even devastation of crop failure. If purchasing from local farmers—through a farmers market, local buying cooperative or Community Supported Agriculture (CSA) farm—we can be part of a growing movement that allows many small family farmers to reclaim their land for growing food, not macadam.

I grew up working in a garden from my earliest days. Gardening is not my favorite work, but I like the way it makes me feel much more in touch with my sisters around the world who also put hoe to ground and grow their own food, and with the women who have lived centuries before me. There is something elemental about the fresh smell of earth in spring, and the color of dirt and weeds staining the hands after pulling pigweed and pruning tomatoes in summer.

There's no escaping that all of this takes hard work, time and energy—and many folks feel they just don't have the time or the desire. I have in my files a typed paragraph from my youngest daughter, Doreen, who hammered it on an old-fashioned type-writer at my office when she was young. Here is what she wrote:

> One day when I was a little girl, I had to go and pull weeds out of the garden. This was not my idea of fun. So I decided to not do my summer chore. Then my mother came home that evening and was not happy that I had not done my job. She scolded me and made me go out that evening and do my chore. The End.

I think she left it on my desk to complain, and even though I winced at the picture of me as a scold, it was probably accurate.

Doreen is now twenty-four, and something funny happened on her way to adulthood: she became a more rabid gardener than her father and me. And that is just great by us. She is currently living at home after graduating from college and working at a nearby bank. Now *she* scolds *me*, and I protest. We should plant herbs, she says (but they never grow for me) or plant squash (but they take over the garden). Doreen wants us to draw out a sketch for the garden (but after thirty-plus years of gardening, somehow we never get around to those sketches anymore). But I am happy to adjust in order to encourage her gardening enthusiasm. She in turn tries not to get carried away with the all-out gardening of our well-known southwestern Virginia resident, novelist Barbara Kingsolver.

In her popular nonfiction book *Animal, Vegetable, Miracle*, Kingsolver details her rural life in which her family vows, for one year, to "buy only food raised in their own neighborhood, grow it themselves, or learn to live without it."[3] For that year, each family member was allowed one free pass to continue buying something that wasn't available locally—something they just didn't want to do without.

Kingsolver admits that she has the advantage of having enough income from her bestsellers to not have to go to a regular nine-to-five job. In any case, it is difficult to garden along with other jobs, but if you look at it as recreation, exercise, and saving money on food, it becomes easier to find the time.

Doreen's interest in gardening was enhanced one summer by volunteering at a neighboring CSA farm run by the Marlin Burkholder family. A CSA offers the opportunity to buy or work for your vegetables and fruits on a subscription plan—paying a monthly fee year-round that helps the farmer to stay in business during the off season, and then receiving boxes of fruits and vegetables each week during the spring, summer, and fall.

I suggested working for the CSA mainly just to give Doreen something to do while she was hunting for paid work. We never expected that she would be abundantly paid in fruits and vegetables, some of which lasted for months, such as bulbs of garlic.

Her harvest was abundant in other ways. She was inspired by the variety of crops they planted (many more kinds of greens than we ever attempted to raise), the new kinds of fruits they traded for their vegetable crops in order to get a variety of items to put into the boxes for their subscribers, and the many different kinds of squash, gourds, and other root crops we knew nothing about.

The CSA work, the Kingsolver book, and her own interest inspired Doreen to go out picking blackberries and raspberries to freeze and use all winter long. She also scolded *me* for buying fruits and vegetables that are not local or in season. I'm sorry, I just can't give up bananas, and they are never going to be local or in season. Even Barbara Kingsolver couldn't give up her coffee from afar.

Almost everyone enjoys picking ripe things from the garden. When kids are old enough to do it adequately is another question, which must be decided with each individual child. And cooking things they have actually grown and babied to maturity—well, for many of us, it is the one way to get kids to eat their vegetables. For example, they can help to chop vegetables for homemade soup.

Especially if you live in a city, you must make an effort to expose your children to where food comes from. *Simply in Season Children's Cookbook* by Mark Beach and Julie Kauffman (Herald Press, 2006) is a beautifully illustrated book that teaches kids the joys and goodness of using locally produced foods in season, whether home grown or purchased, whenever possible. Gardens, whether vegetable, flower, or potted patio plants, keep us more in touch with the cycles of nature, the rhythms of creation, and the goodness of God, who sends rain on the just and the unjust, the deserving and the undeserving. And when the rains come and the tomatoes ripen and the first plate of steaming-hot sweet corn is put on the table, we feel much more gratitude to God for making it all possible.

For a list of CSAs in the United States, go to http://www.localharvest.org/csa/. And for more on Kingsolver's farm/garden and recipes, go to http://animalvegetablemiracle.org/.

● ● ● ● ● ● ● ● ● ● ●

Spinach-Tomato Quiche

Rebecca Thatcher Murcia

The whole family can chip in to make this ode to the summer's harvest. The next time you have company coming, plan to get your children washing spinach, grating cheese, and beating eggs to make this quiche with a rich, complex flavor. Small children especially enjoy assembling the layers.

1 homemade or store-bought pie crust
1½ cup / 375 ml (packed) Swiss cheese, shredded
2 tablespoons olive oil
1 small onion, chopped
3 cloves garlic, minced
½–1 pound / 250–500 g spinach
4 large eggs, beaten
1 cup / 250 ml milk
1 teaspoon salt

1 tablespoon fresh basil, chopped (or 1 teaspoon dried)

½ teaspoon celery seed

½ teaspoon dry mustard

½ teaspoon curry powder

½ teaspoon onion powder

Pinch of cayenne

Pinch of nutmeg

2 medium tomatoes, sliced or chopped

½ tablespoon fresh basil chopped (or ½ teaspoon dried)

Preheat oven to 350° F / 180° C. Place the dough in a 9- or 10-inch deep-dish pie pan, and pierce it in several places to avoid big bubbles. Bake for 9 minutes.

Meanwhile, sauté onions and garlic in olive oil for 3–5 minutes or until onion is translucent. Add the spinach and continue to sauté until spinach is wilted. Set spinach mixture aside.

Mix together the eggs, milk, and seasonings, and set aside.

Spread half the shredded cheese over the bottom of the pie crust, then top it with the spinach mixture. Layer the remaining cheese over the spinach. Pour the egg and milk mixture evenly over the top. Top with tomato slices or chunks, and sprinkle them with basil. Bake for 1½ hours.

Pasta Fresca

Carmen Wyse

This is the meal we wait all year for and the first thing we make when the tomatoes start to come in. My son's birthday is at the end of July, and he frequently requests this for his birthday meal.

4–6 large tomatoes, chopped (about 4 cups / 1 L)
6–8 large fresh basil leaves
2–3 large garlic cloves, minced
1 tablespoon extra virgin olive oil
Salt and pepper to taste
1 pound / 500 g pasta
½ pound / 250 g fresh mozzarella cheese, cut into ½-inch / 1 cm cubes
Parmesan cheese, grated (optional)

Set aside 1 cup of the chopped tomatoes and 2 basil leaves. In a blender or food processor, puree the remaining tomatoes and basil with the garlic and olive oil until smooth. Add salt and pepper to taste.

Cook the pasta until al dente, according to package directions. Cut the reserved basil leaves into strips. Drain the cooked pasta, and toss it immediately with the mozzarella cubes. Add the sauce, and mix well. Top with the reserved tomatoes, basil, and grated cheese, if desired. Serve immediately.

Green Beans Wrapped in Bacon

Burton Buller

When garden green beans are in season, this recipe offers a delicious alternative to steamed green beans, as good as they are. Great when hosting dinner at your table.

2 pounds / 1 kg fresh green beans
6 slices bacon, cut in half
4 tablespoons butter, melted
3 tablespoons brown sugar
⅛ teaspoon garlic powder
Salt and pepper to taste

Preheat oven to 350° F / 180° C. Cook beans in boiling salted water for 3 minutes. Drain. Separate beans into 12 bundles. Wrap a piece of bacon around the middle of each bundle. Place bundles in a buttered 9x13-inch baking dish.

Melt butter and brown sugar in a small saucepan. Drizzle over the green bean bundles. Sprinkle with garlic powder, salt, and pepper. Bake for 20–30 minutes or until bacon is slightly crisp.

Asian Love Salad

Zachary Taylor

Prepare salad:
1 6-ounce / 180 g bag baby spinach leaves
1 cup / 250 ml shredded carrots
1 cup / 250 ml diced celery
1 cup / 250 ml sliced mushrooms
1 cup / 250 ml thawed frozen peas
1¼ cup / 300 ml cashews

Place all ingredients in large bowl, layered in the order above, and keep it cool. This can be prepared early and kept until ready to serve. Do not mix dressing and hot rice until ready to serve.

Prepare dressing:
⅔ cup / 150 ml extra virgin olive oil
⅔ cup / 150 ml low-sodium soy sauce
2 cloves garlic, crushed or minced
1½ teaspoons black ground pepper

Combine dressing ingredients in a jar or container at room temperature until ready to serve. Separation is normal.

Prepare rice:
1 cup / 250 ml brown rice

Cook 1 cup / 250 ml brown rice in 2 cups / 500 ml boiling water (should make around 2 cups / 500 ml cooked). White rice works too.

Serve:
When ready to serve, make sure rice is hot, and mix it into the salad. Stir or shake dressing to mix ingredients, and pour over everything. Stir until everything is mixed and spinach has wilted. Serve warm as a side dish. Very good warmed up as well.

Broccoli Salad

Melodie Davis

There are many recipes for broccoli salad. This is a basic one, which came from a friend of a friend, Joyce Thomas. Even people who think they don't like broccoli salad seem to love this.

In large bowl, combine:
1 large head of broccoli, or several crowns, chopped (substitute
    half cauliflower, if you like)
⅓ cup / 75 ml of raisins or dried cranberries
3 spring onions, chopped (or ¼–½ cup chopped red onion)
4 slices of bacon, fried and crumbled
½ cup / 125 ml chopped pecans, almonds, sunflower seeds,
    peanuts, or walnuts (optional)

Dressing:
1 cup / 250 ml salad dressing (such as Miracle Whip)
1–2 tablespoons vinegar (to your taste)
¼ cup / 50 ml sugar

Stir dressing ingredients together and pour over the salad. Best if refrigerated several hours or overnight.

Greek Zucchini Cakes

Carmen Wyse

We love Greek food, and this recipe uses a lot of Greek flavors and a lot of zucchini that might be piling up in the middle of summer. Serve it as a side with something grilled and fresh corn on the cob, and you have the perfect summer meal.

1 pound / 500 g zucchini, grated
1 teaspoon kosher salt (¾ teaspoon regular salt)
¾ cup / 175 ml crumbled feta
2 large eggs, beaten
3 green onions, sliced
⅓ cup / 75 ml flour
¼ cup / 50 ml chopped pine nuts (substitute almonds or walnuts)
1 tablespoon chopped fresh dill (1 teaspoon dried)
1½ teaspoon chopped fresh oregano (½ teaspoon dried)
2–3 garlic cloves, diced
Fresh ground pepper

Combine grated zucchini and salt. Let set 5 minutes (no more, or it will get mushy). Rinse in cold water and wring out in a towel.

Combine dry zucchini with everything else. Form into small patties and sauté in olive oil until browned, about 3 minutes per side. Serve immediately.

Raspberry Poppy Seed Dressing

Kimberly Metzler

I tried a raspberry poppy-seed dressing at Bear Trap Farm in Mount Solon, Virginia, during one of my husband's work Christmas parties. After hearing me talk about it, a friend made up this recipe for me.

⅓ cup / 75 ml red wine vinegar
⅓ cup / 75 ml canola oil
⅛ cup / 25 ml sugar (or Splenda)
2 tablespoons red raspberry jam
1 teaspoon salt
½ teaspoon pepper
1 small onion, chopped
2 teaspoons poppy seeds

Blend all but the poppy seeds in a blender until smooth. Stir in poppy seeds. Refrigerate.

Sour Cream Berry Pie

Carmen Wyse

This is an old recipe that's been in my family for years—it's shown up in two of our family cookbooks, and a version of it can be found in the Simply in Season *cookbook as well. The original recipe calls for blackberries, but any summer fruit (singly or in a combination) works well here. If you use berries or rhubarb, keep the full cup of sugar; if you use peaches or another particularly sweet fruit, you might want to decrease the sugar somewhat.*

2½ cups / 625 ml berries or other fruit
1 cup / 250 ml sugar
2 tablespoons flour
1 cup / 250 ml sour cream

Preheat oven to 450° F / 230° C.

Wash berries (or other fruit) and place in an unbaked pie crust. Combine sugar and flour. Add sour cream and blend thoroughly. Pour mixture over fruit. Bake for 15 minutes. Reduce heat to 350° F / 180° C and continue to bake for another 30 minutes.

3

• • • • • • • • •

Work: The Real Enemy of Families

We hear a lot about forces that are destroying the family. Television. Divorce. Radical left-wingers. Pro-choicers.

How about work schedules? When our daughter Michelle was sixteen, she started her first real job part time—and I had a small mothering crisis. It wasn't quite the empty nest, but when she went off to work, I felt bereft: I missed her a whole lot more than when she was with her friends or at school or at some activity. I felt like I was the one who should be going off to work instead of my child.

And suddenly our lives, especially evening mealtimes, were more fractured than ever. The employer wants your child to work Sunday afternoon—and suddenly it sinks in with Dad that Sunday afternoon drives with the family for a hike in the mountains or a float down a river will be even less frequent. And so I have come to think that work—actually jobs—are a real destroyer of family life.

Of course we need jobs to survive, but it isn't only paid work that pulls the family in many directions: it is the over-scheduling of children and families. Many times, if you have three kids or more, planning the evening rat race of getting them to three or more activities requires a computer program and a fleet of chauffeurs (or carpoolers). How did I ever do all that without texting, let alone a cell phone? And how do we manage to preserve family mealtime in such a scenario?

First we parents need to pay attention to the role that work takes in our own lives. How do we find a good balance between family life and employed life? Here are some questions to ask:

1. Does my work schedule automatically take precedence over my family schedule, including mealtime? There are times when we must give up family priorities to meet deadlines or special demands at work. But if we are being asked to work extensive overtime, travel out of town frequently, work weekends, or move to another state or province for our job, these are times when we must consider family priorities. Sometimes work should probably win (to keep employers happy and to keep jobs), but families definitely need to win the schedule war at times as well. It is hard to keep family mealtime when Dad or Mom is always getting home at 9:00 p.m.

2. Am I using work to escape an unhappy or stressful situation at home, anything from a colicky baby to a depressed spouse to teens who are coming home after midnight? While it is a wonderful gift to enjoy work, if you find yourself staying extra hours because you know the kids will be quietly put to bed by the time you get home, you need to ask whether you are working to escape stress at home.

3. Can I be upfront with my employer about what I will or will not do? Many firms honor employee preferences, such as longstanding attendance at religious services on weekends. If family demands make travel difficult, be clear about that.

4. Can I work part time and still make ends meet? Anyone with children at home—I don't care what age they are—will benefit from the flexibility afforded by part-time hours. When my kids were finally all in school, I thought maybe I should work full time, but I soon discovered that teens—not just toddlers—benefit from having a parent available some of the time. How much money do we

really need? My experience and that of countless others I know is that we usually manage to get by on what we make no matter how little it is, and we manage to spend whatever additional we earn. Giving up a few hours of work in exchange for time with family is usually a choice you'll value. And it also makes family mealtime much more doable.

5. Do teens really need a job? In spite of the extra stressor to the family schedule, we welcomed our kids picking up more of their expenses with money that came from something else besides Mom and Dad's budget. Their working contributed in a good way to our family's economic situation. But saving up big funds for college wasn't a goal, especially because we knew they would need to apply for financial aid for college, and kids' personal savings frequently count against them. While holding down a part-time job may offer life lessons for teens, families need to guard against teens working just to buy the latest electronic gizmo or designer jeans.

What about over-scheduled kids? It begins with swimming classes for infants (yes, we did that), music appreciation for toddlers, ballet, karate, piano lessons, Little League—you know the list. Children often like to explore many different activities, but parents need to be on guard against pushing their kids into too many. Is it something they want to do or something *you* want them to do?

I'll never forget my wake-up call when I encouraged our oldest to try out for basketball when she got to sixth grade. I had a great time playing basketball in middle school, high school, and college. She was quite tall for her age, so she gamely gave it a try. But her peers had been playing competitively since first or second grade. She was five years behind and never did catch up. Luckily, she found her own thing—band—something my husband and I never participated in. Not only her but her sisters' high school lives revolved around their band and choral experiences, and one of them made a career in music. So we made many family sacrifices for and around band: countless 4:00 a.m. band chicken barbecues (more on this later); private music lessons; band trips. But at least they weren't doing band *and* basketball *and* theater *and* tap all at once.

Finally, as you weigh your family's involvements, one other thing that can suffer is volunteer time. When we are working ten, twelve, or fourteen hours a day and trying to keep up with family activities, there is literally no time or energy to volunteer for church or civic activities. Thus our *extended* families and communities suffer because of our tendency to overwork and our over-scheduling of children. We don't have time to visit elderly aunts or lonely widowers. We don't have time to mow the church lawn or help serve the homeless. We don't have time to get the family together for dinner.

● ● ● ● ● ● ● ● ●

Jesus had much to say on the topic of putting priority on the important things in life. His parable of the rich fool ties nicely into our reflections on food. In Luke 12:13-21 Jesus tells this parable to respond to someone in the crowd who said (and I hear a slightly mocking or joking-but-serious tone here), "Tell my brother to divide the inheritance with me." Jesus responds in kind: "Man, who appointed me a judge or an arbiter between you?"

But then Jesus goes on to tell this parable: The ground of a rich man produced a good crop, and as he considered what to do, he decided to tear down his barns and build bigger ones to store all his grain and goods. (Perhaps so far so good. Isn't this just wise planning?) But then the kicker comes with the rich fool contemplating, "Now I will take life easy: eat, drink, and be merry."

And God's response in Jesus' story is "'You fool, this very night your life will be demanded from you. Then who will get what you have prepared for yourself?' This is how it will be with anyone who stores up things for himself but is not rich toward God" (vv. 20-21).

The point is almost too easy: what will all our activities,

schedules, and overwork get us if we do not pay attention to godly priorities? Jesus turns the subject from inheritance and things to our attitudes toward them. We also must not overlook the implied inequity: here was a rich guy planning on hoarding his grain when certainly there were poor folks who could have used some, even a *portion* or a tithe of his crop.

As we weigh all our interests, concerns, and priorities, it is often hard to find balance. Keeping our hearts and minds focused on the end goal—ourselves and our families as true children of God and servants of Jesus, rather than slaves to our schedules—will help to keep priorities in line.

This chapter includes recipes to help your family eat nutritiously in a minimum of time—one-dish meals that you can make ahead on weekends and freeze, or whip up in a quick half-hour after work. In the next chapter, we'll explore "portable home-cooked fast food" options when you don't even have time for any of the above.

●　●　●　●　●　●　●　●　●　●

Weeknight Paella

Jodi Nisly Hertzler

This is a relatively easy one-dish meal that tastes much more complicated than it is. Even my picky children like it. Experiment with different meats and veggies to find your favorite combination.

4 cups / 1 L chicken stock
1 teaspoon turmeric
3 tablespoons olive oil
1 medium onion, diced
2 cups / 500 ml white rice
Salt and freshly ground pepper
2 cups / 500 ml raw peeled shrimp, cut into ½-inch / 1 cm chunks
        (substitute scallops, pork, chicken)
1 cup / 250 ml sausage, cut into small pieces (kielbasa or chorizo
        recommended)
½–1 cup / 125–250 ml vegetables of your choice (I usually use
        peas or edamame and chopped fresh spinach)
Minced parsley (for garnish)

Preheat oven to 500° F / 260° C. Warm the stock in a saucepan or microwave, along with the turmeric.

Warm oil in an ovenproof 12-inch skillet (I use cast-iron) over medium-high heat. Add onion and cook, stirring occasionally, until translucent, about 5 minutes.

Add the rice and cook, stirring frequently, until glossy, 1–2 minutes. Season liberally with salt and pepper, and add the warmed stock. Stir in the shrimp, sausage, and vegetables. Transfer skillet to the oven. Bake about 25 minutes until all the liquid is absorbed and the rice is dry on top. Garnish with parsley, and serve immediately.

Pizza Casserole

Sheri Hartzler

This dish was the standard "what to feed the soccer team" meal when my boys were growing up. It combines the taste of a pizza with some good-for-them pasta and is easy to double and triple as needed, depending on the number of people showing up to eat.

8 ounces (4 cups) / 1 L uncooked ½-inch / 1 cm noodles
½ pound / 250 g bulk mild sausage
¾ pound / 375 g hamburger
¼ cup / 50 ml chopped onions
2 tablespoons chopped pimento-stuffed olives
1 can (4 oz.) / 115 g chopped mushrooms
¼ cup / 50 ml mushroom liquid
1 can (8 oz.) / 240 g pizza sauce
2 cups plus 2 tablespoons shredded cheddar cheese

Preheat oven to 350° F / 180° C. Cook noodles as directed, then rinse and drain. Cook meat and onion until brown, and drain well. Drain mushrooms, saving ¼ cup of liquid. In a mixing bowl, toss together noodles, meat mixture, mushrooms and liquid, olives, 2 cups cheddar cheese, and pizza sauce. Pour into a 2-quart casserole. Bake for 20–25 minutes. Sprinkle with 2 tablespoons cheese for the last 10 minutes.

Variation: Can be heated in a slow cooker on low for 1–2 hours.

Southern Fried Catfish

Kimberly Metzler

My husband fell in love with catfish when we were in Mennonite Voluntary Service in Jackson, Mississippi. We asked a friend for the recipe when they served us this main dish.

Have ready:

Catfish

Beaten egg

Mix together equal parts of cornmeal and flour. Sprinkle in salt and pepper to taste. Dip catfish into the beaten egg and then dip into the cornmeal mixture. Fry fish in canola or peanut oil in a skillet over medium heat until browned (about 4 minutes per side).

Barbeque Spareribs or Pork Chops

Melodie Davis

This is an easy, oven-baked way to cook any kind of pork you wish. The recipe came from my sister-in-law, Barbara Davis, from whom I gratefully learned to cook many "Virginian" dishes. I frequently make these with some form of oven potatoes, since the oven is on anyway (see Oven French Fries recipe on page 70).

3–4 spareribs or 5–6 pork chops or tenderloin pieces
¾ cup / 175 ml ketchup
¾ cup / 175 ml water
2 tablespoons Worcestershire sauce
½ teaspoon pepper
1 teaspoon paprika
2 tablespoons vinegar
1 teaspoon chili powder
Salt to taste

Cook spareribs in salted water until half done, about 15 minutes. Meanwhile, mix all other ingredients together and heat in a small saucepan. When ribs are half done, place in a 9x13-inch baking dish. Pour sauce over pork. Bake at 350° F / 180° C for 30–45 minutes, turning once and ladling sauce on top of ribs or pork chops.

Oven French Fries

Melodie Davis

This is a recipe from Elva Honeyager, who was a cook at my elementary school in Middlebury, Indiana, and a neighbor of ours. For my own family, I started with this basic recipe, but in more recent years I've used olive oil instead of butter or margarine. These can also be cooked in a pan on the grill for yet another taste. As "homemade" potato chips or oven fries, these are a special treat.

3–4 medium potatoes
¼ cup / 50 ml margarine or oil
Seasoning to taste

Preheat oven to 450° F / 230° C. Peel and cut raw potatoes into slices about ¼-inch thick. Cover potatoes with water in a saucepan and cover. Bring slices to a boil on top of stove; cook about 5 minutes, only until they are partially done.

Meanwhile, melt margarine or heat olive oil in the preheating oven in a baking dish (baking dish with low sides, 9x13-inch or larger). Drain potatoes and carefully place them in a single layer in the baking dish. Bake for 10–12 minutes. Turn each potato slice and bake 5–8 more minutes until they look good and crusty.

Variations: Leave peels on. Use Lawry's seasoned salt, Mrs. Dash, paprika, or just salt and pepper. Try sea salt and chopped fresh or dried herbs, such as rosemary, thyme, or oregano.

La Madeleine Restaurant's Famous Tomato Basil Soup

Natalie Francisco

After visiting the French restaurant and baker La Madeleine in Houston years ago with my husband, I fell in love with their tomato basil soup. It was the best I had ever tasted. Since we could not obtain the recipe from the staff there, my husband found it online, and we determined to make it ourselves. To my utter delight, it tasted exactly the same as the soup at La Madeleine.

4 cups / 1 L fresh tomatoes, cored, peeled, and chopped (8–10),
        or canned whole tomatoes, crushed
4 cups / 1 L tomato juice (or part vegetable or chicken stock)
12–14 basil leaves, washed fresh, and coarsely chopped
1 cup / 250 ml heavy cream
¼ pound / 125 g sweet unsalted butter
Salt to taste
¼ teaspoon cracked black pepper
Lemon juice (optional)

Combine tomatoes with juice or stock in saucepan. Simmer 30 minutes. Add basil leaves, then puree in small batches in blender or food processor (or better yet, use a hand-held food blender, right in the cooking pan). Return to saucepan and add cream and butter while stirring over low heat. Garnish with basil leaves, and serve with your favorite bread.

Note: if the soup tastes too acidic, stir in about 1 tablespoon brown sugar.

Parmesan Chicken Burgers

Jodi Nisly Hertzler

I came up with these as an alternative to the highly processed frozen chicken patties in the store. I like to make a double batch and freeze leftovers. Thawed in the microwave or a toaster oven, they make a tasty, quick lunch.

Breading:
2 slices wheat bread, diced
½ cup / 125 ml finely grated Parmesan cheese
1 tablespoon chopped fresh parsley

Blend bread, Parmesan, and parsley in food processor to fine crumbs. Pour into a pie dish and set aside.

Mix together:
1 pound / 500 g ground chicken (white meat)
2–3 tablespoons finely diced or grated onion
1–3 cloves garlic, pressed
1 teaspoon chopped fresh parsley
½ tablespoon olive oil
1 teaspoon salt
Pepper to taste

Shape the chicken mixture into ½-inch thick patties, then coat with crumbs. They're sticky, but form as you pat them in the crumbs.

Heat 1½ tablespoons olive oil in a large, nonstick skillet over medium heat. Cook patties until nicely browned and cooked through, about 4 minutes per side.

Makes 4–6 patties, depending on how big you make them. Serve on Whole Wheat Rolls (recipe in chapter 1).

4

• • • • • • • • •

Eating on the Run—
Taking Charge of "Fast" Food

It started with what I call "excavating ancient ruins": cleaning out the family minivan. While the children were in their busiest years and before any of them started driving, I cleaned the minivan about every two or three weeks, and it always astonished me how much stuff accumulated there. One day in early December, I took inventory:

- A stadium chair, to watch our oldest daughter in marching band at football games.
- Assorted blankets and raincoats for comfort while watching said performances as the season grew ever colder and meaner.
- A bird-watching book and binoculars, for impromptu fall hikes with spectacular mountain views.
- Scissors used in wrapping a gift purchased on the way to a birthday party.
- Books.
- Sunday school papers. Memos about youth group.
- Flashlights. A fly swatter. A sunshade for the front window (instantly bringing back warm beach memories).

- Dried up French fries and unused ketchup packs. Straw wrappers. From all those meals grabbed on the go to somewhere else.

If you sealed your family car in a time capsule at any given moment, and someone opened it fifty years from now, the items preserved there would be a good picture of the routines that make up your life.

Many of us feel we almost spend more time in our cars than at home. No wonder our vehicles accumulate so much stuff from our lives. If you have a baby, your car likely contains spilled Cheerios, a pack of wipes, rattles, a toy or three. And, of course, the everlasting car seat. I thought we would *always* have a car seat in our car, especially with three children. Now, in many localities, children use seats or boosters until they are seven or eight.

I've heard that the French don't eat in their cars; my daughter, who has friends from Paris, confirms this. I admire those who have the discipline and take the time to dine in a more civilized fashion. But so often eating while driving, especially on trips, is not only a great time saver, it also helps ease the boredom of the trip.

Many of us spend up to two to three hours a day in our vehicles, even if we don't have a long work commute. The Answers.com website puts the average at three hours a day; commuting, running children to activities, your own activities, shopping, errands, and church involvements all add up. My kids' high school was eleven miles away, and the oldest took a jazz class that met before the bus ran. Before she got her license, if there were other before- and after-school activities, I sometimes ended up driving sixty-six miles a day, just running kids.

Back when we had three kids under the age of five, I sometimes felt our youngest spent more time napping in the car than she did in her crib. I would pick up the oldest from nursery school and by the time we got there, the baby would drift off every time. Then we would do errands, and she would go to sleep again. Soon someone would be hungry, and we'd succumb to the lure of the Golden Arches.

Does eating on the run have to mean bad nutrition? It probably does unless we are careful and take charge. The fat calories and thin nutrition of a Happy Meal soon give way, especially if you have boys, to ever-larger "super size" portions. The excesses of the fast-food industry are well known and exposed in documentaries like *Super Size Me*, as are our nutritional failures in *King Corn*. Corn subsidies paid by the government to farmers have helped lead to high production of corn, which is turned into high-fructose corn syrup, corn-fed meat, and corn-based processed foods—all of which aren't good for our health and waistlines. Triple burgers topped by cheese, bacon, and mayo are over the top in every way, when a good basic burger with lettuce and tomato (and okay, a little mayo) has half the calorie count and tastes better if you train yourself that way.

Having grown up in the fifties and having lived through the early McDonald's era, I have not weaned myself off fast-food hamburgers. But I do look for ways not to yield to the temptation of such fast calories packed away without real enjoyment. I have discovered creative alternatives that offer more opportunities for family fun and interaction than always settling for the same old.

Packed picnics take a bit of work and planning ahead, but they are a great way to buck the trend of fast food. When my Miller family traveled in the days before fast food, we often had on-the-spot picnics purchased from a local grocery in whatever town we were passing through. The whole family would traipse into the grocery store, and each member would get to pick out one favorite item to add to the lunch: bread, cold meat, cheese, lettuce, chips, a quart of juice, apples or bananas, and (heaven help us) Twinkies. Okay, so that wasn't exactly a five-star nutritious meal either, but it was much better than most fast-food meals today. It was fun and a treat, though it didn't always save money, and Mom had to guard against us running up the bill even more with extra treats.

My father used to work long hours in the field during planting or harvesting seasons. Often we would carry supper to him in the field, and sometimes Mom would make it a family affair if the day or week had been particularly long and we needed some family togetherness. The menu was simple: fried-egg sandwiches (sometimes with bacon or ham), celery or carrot sticks, maybe some chips, a cookie, an apple, and water. We wrapped the sandwiches in foil, and they were often only lukewarm and somewhat soggy by the time we ate them. But the taste was sublime as we sat on the edge of the field with the scent of freshly turned sod in our nostrils and the diesel fumes of the tractor lending their own aroma.

But what I truly savor about those times was the family adventure they afforded: breaking out of the routine, being with Dad, playing in the fresh dirt, and getting out of the house. And that's what the creative ideas in this chapter for "portable meals on the road" have going for them too.

Another illustration from the Bible of food on the go is the story of the boy who shared his lunch of five loaves and two fish (Mark 6:30-44). Children's storybooks often have the mother packing the boy's lunch the day Jesus stretched it to feed the 5,000. But maybe it was the boy's own self-reliance that had him grab quickly a little grub from the house as he dashed off to hear the famous teacher. It is that kind of self-reliance I'd like to focus on here. I never got to the place of my kids packing their own lunches while they were in school, but somehow they all got there as adults. They all choose the frugality of a packed lunch on most days rather than eating out while at their office jobs. But Jodi's great list of food options for lunches should make it easier for any family to work toward that goal of self-reliance for kids.

You can make portable picnics as creative and environmentally friendly as you like, using reusable bottles for drinks, homemade bread for sandwiches, and fruits and vegetables. The cooler can also be used when you buy meats, cheeses, veggies, or fruit in a grocery. If a farmers market happens to be open where you trek, obviously that offers many more nutritious and fresh choices. Keep a box or basket in your car with basic supplies like paper towels, utensils, cups, or plates.

Even when you fly, since airlines no longer offer much free food, it is acceptable to whip out your own homemade sandwich or salad, as long as you pay attention to the carry-on guidelines du jour.

We can take charge of a fast-food habit. Use fast food as necessary to survive and sometimes just because you like it, but don't let it take over your life, your family, or your waistline.

● ● ● ● ● ● ● ● ● ●

Making a Lunchbox Menu

Jodi Nisly Hertzler

In an attempt to get my children more involved in helping to pack their school lunches, I devised a chart to hang on the refrigerator. The chart provided a list of foods in four categories: proteins, grains, fruits/vegetables, and treats/ extras. I instructed them to include at least one thing from each of the first three categories, more than one from the fruits/vegetables list, and only one from the treats/extras list. The list comes in handy anytime we need to pack food to take anywhere. It is also a good way to teach some basic nutrition (learning what proteins are, and figuring out that leftover macaroni and cheese combined two categories, for instance). The following is a similar list to spur your own ideas. Items such as waffles or refried beans might seem unappetizing to some of us to eat cold, but most kids love the idea of dunking waffle sticks into a little container of syrup or eating a room-temperature bean and cheese burrito.

Proteins	Grains	Fruits/Vegetables	Treats/Extras
Peanut butter	Bread	Apple	Chips
Turkey	Crackers (whole grain)	Grapes	Pretzels
Ham	Noodles	Banana	Cookies*
Salami	Muffin*	Peaches	Pudding*
Hard-boiled egg	Granola bar*	Pears	Syrup (for dipping waffles)
Yogurt	Waffle sticks*	Oranges	Dip for veggies
Cheese	Healthy cereals	Plums	Popcorn balls*
Nuts	Tortilla*	Berries	
Kielbasa chunks	Whole wheat bagel	Dried fruit/fruit leather*	
Refried beans	Pancake	Applesauce	
Cream cheese		Carrot sticks	
		Celery sticks	
		Cucumber slices	
Leftovers		Cherry tomatoes	
		Broccoli	
		Cauliflower	
		Bell pepper strips	
		Salsa*	

* Recipes for these items can be found in this book.

Chewy Granola Bars

Jodi Nisly Hertzler

I like these granola bars more than some I've tried, because they remain chewy, and they are easy to cut into bars and freeze. If you like your granola bars crunchy, simply bake them for a few minutes. Toss frozen granola bars in lunchboxes or picnic bags for a nutritious snack.

2 cups / 500 ml old-fashioned oatmeal
1 cup / 250 ml sliced or slivered almonds
1 cup / 250 ml shredded coconut
½ cup / 125 ml toasted wheat germ
¼ cup / 50 ml flax meal (optional)
3 tablespoons butter
½ cup / 125 ml honey
½ cup / 125 ml peanut butter
¼ cup / 50 ml brown sugar
2 teaspoons vanilla extract
¼ teaspoon salt
½–1½ cup / 125–375 ml dried fruit (cranberries, raisins, chopped
        apricots, chopped pitted dates, etc.)

Preheat the oven to 350° F / 180° C. Grease an 8x12-inch baking dish, and line it with parchment paper.

Toss the oatmeal, almonds, and coconut together on a sheet pan, and bake for 10–12 minutes, stirring occasionally until lightly browned. Transfer the mixture to a large mixing bowl, and stir in the wheat germ and flax meal.

Place the butter, honey, peanut butter, brown sugar, vanilla, and salt in a small saucepan, and bring to a boil over medium heat. Cook and stir for a minute. Pour over the toasted oatmeal mixture. Add the dried fruit and stir well.

Pour the mixture into the greased pan. Wet your fingers and press the mixture evenly into the pan. (For crunchy bars, bake in a 300° F / 150° C oven for about 15 minutes, until light golden brown.) Cool completely (2–3 hours, if you baked them), then use the parchment paper to lift the mixture out of the pan. Cut into squares.

Fruit Leather

Carmen Wyse and Jodi Nisly Hertzler

Fruit leather makes an easy snack on the go, or a simple addition to a packed lunch. There are many variations you can experiment with.

2 cups / 500 ml applesauce or any fruit puree
1–4 tablespoons honey (optional)

Preheat oven to its lowest setting: 140° to 150° F / 60° to 65° C. Line a cookie sheet (one with a lip) with tin foil, and spray with nonstick cooking spray. Pour the fruit puree onto the cookie sheet and spread it thin. Put in oven, leaving oven door propped open just a bit (I use a wooden spoon). Bake overnight, or at least 8 hours, until the leather is flexible but no longer sticky. Lift foil off the cookie sheet and peel off the leather. Cut into strips (a pizza cutter works well) and roll the strips up. (Optional: cut into squares). Store in a plastic bag or airtight container.

Gorilla Bars

Jodi Nisly Hertzler

*My three-year-old son adores store-bought, fruit-filled granola bars (he
calls them "gorilla bars"), but I have mixed feelings spending money
on these preservative-laden treats. I found a recipe for this homemade
version on the Internet and adapted it to decrease fat and increase the
whole grains and protein. My children (and other kids who have tried
my experiments) enjoy them when made with 100-percent whole wheat
flour; adult friends think that makes them too "floury" and prefer some
white flour mixed in. So adapt this recipe to your family's preference.*

1 cup / 250 ml butter, softened (or ½ cup butter and ½ cup
    applesauce)
1 cup / 250 ml brown sugar
½ teaspoon salt
1 cup / 250 ml whole wheat flour
1 cup / 250 ml all-purpose flour (substitute whole wheat flour for
    part or all of the white)
1½ cup / 375 ml quick oats
½ cup / 125 ml finely ground nuts, such as pecan meal (optional,
    but these improve flavor and add protein)
1 teaspoon vanilla or almond extract
10 ounces (approx. 1 cup) / 300 g fruit preserves or apple butter

Preheat oven to 350° F / 180° C. Cream butter and sugar. (If you're
substituting applesauce for some of the butter, add it now and mix to
blend.) Add dry ingredients, one at a time, mixing well after each. Mix
in vanilla or almond extract. Press half of the mixture into a greased
9x13-inch pan. Spread evenly with preserves.

Dump remaining crumb mixture on a piece of parchment or wax paper,
and top with another piece of wax paper. Use a rolling pin to press

mixture out into a 9x13-inch rectangle, using the pan as a guide. Peel off the top piece, and use the bottom piece to flip the mixture over on top of the preserves. Press gently to adhere topping to preserves, using fingers to trim edges and cover holes. (This method is optional. You can just press the topping on by hand, but I find that this method solidifies the mixture nicely and keeps the bar layers intact, making the result more like the store-bought variety.)

Bake for 20–25 minutes, until edges turn golden brown. Cool completely before cutting into bars.

Peanut Butter Popcorn Balls

Lois Priest

This is a recipe I found on a weekly news sheet my son brought home from school his kindergarten year. These are soft and not sticky like popcorn balls made from corn syrup. We love them! They make a great lunchbox or after-school treat.

½ cup / 125 ml honey
½ cup / 125 ml brown sugar
½ cup / 125 ml peanut butter
1 bag popped microwave popcorn with unpopped kernels
    removed

In a saucepan, mix honey, brown sugar, and peanut butter, and heat to boiling point (but do *not* boil). Remove from heat and pour over popcorn, stirring to coat well. Shape into balls.

Variation: leave in clusters, instead of shaping into balls.

5

• • • • • • • • •

Comfort Foods and Memories: Macaroni and Cheese and Saturday Night Hamburgers

I had fantasized about it for years. *Thirty-five* years to be exact. I had drooled over the memory of a Jonah Club Fish Fry that long. Such events are well known in Indiana, where I grew up, and seem to have originated there about 1935. Anyway, I jumped at the chance to go to one of these fundraising dinners when family business took me to Indiana and happened to coincide with the date of the fish fry at my old high school.

When I walked into the gymnasium at Bethany Christian High School, where the dinner was served, all the old smells came rushing back: a delicious mingling of distant French fry oil and mild fish, freshly baked homemade pies, potato chips, plain white bread, coleslaw (the sugar-and-vinegar kind), with a little lingering gymnasium smell as well. Now, that may not sound inviting, but put that mix of smells together and it's like walking into your mother's or grandmother's kitchen to sniff your favorite childhood meal, welcoming you home.

I think I enjoyed those fish fries so much as a kid because it was one of the few times a year our family ate out—other than on vacations. My earliest memories of the dinners go back long before I had ever gone to my first McDonald's and years before the advent of places like Long John Silvers and Captain D's.

Now you can guess the rest of the story. When I attended the recent fry, thirty-five years later, the fish was good but disappointing. I had forgotten that the fish pieces were square, and somehow this was a big deal. They were little more than frozen fish patties, deep fried in fat and offered to you any time your plate emptied. The memory of it was much better than the actual taste.

I wonder if Esau had that kind of disappointing food memory experience when he craved a good bowl of "red stew." Genesis 25 tells us that Jacob was cooking some stew when Esau came in from having been out hunting without bringing home any game. He was famished. He said, "Quick, let me have some of that red stew!" (The Bible adds that this is why Esau was also called "Edom," because *Edom* means red.) Later the Bible describes the dish as lentil stew with bread. Yum!

Whatever the recipe, Esau was so desperate, or so given to quick satisfaction of desires, that he swore his birthright to his twin brother, Jacob, who was younger by just minutes.

It may have tasted good in that moment, but later Esau surely regretted his quick sale. But in his moment of hunger, the memory of the food and the delicious smell combined to make the food irresistible: something he had to have.

Esau's deal also says a lot about Esau, his relationship to his brother and his family, and everything we don't want to be: given to satisfying physical cravings, quick to despise or deny our heritage, tossing away our family blessing for a bowl of soup. Today we would probably describe Jacob and Esau's family as dysfunctional, what with Rebekah doting on Jacob, Isaac's favoritism toward Esau, and an extreme jealousy between brothers that started in the womb.

Memories associated with food are an important part of our experiences as families—whether happy or not. A good question to ponder is whether it is the food or the people associated with the food that makes the memories.

As I was growing up, our normal menu for Saturday night

was plain hamburgers fried in a skillet (or occasionally grilled in summer), fresh buns, dill pickles, potato chips, and for dessert, ice cream. That simple menu was a staple; if we deviated or were invited away, someone could be counted on to say, "It just doesn't seem like Saturday night without hamburgers." Mom would occasionally switch out the burgers for sloppy joes. The hamburger was always wonderful ground beef from our own or a neighbor's cattle, but Mom didn't believe in "spoiling hamburgers by dolling them up" with onions, seasonings, or marinades.

When I tried to initiate the tradition of Saturday night burgers with my own husband and children, it just didn't work with our lifestyle. None of my siblings have kept that tradition either. I would more often have hamburgers through the week as a quick, after-work meal that was sure to please all tastes, and I would spend more time on weekends cooking bigger meals when I had time. I came to appreciate why my mom liked that particular tradition so well: Saturday was one night she didn't have to plan what to make for dinner. It was just a given.

New generations can begin and treasure their own comfort foods, menus, or traditions. When our children were still small, I started whipping up "homemade" cinnamon rolls on Sunday morning, using canned biscuit dough, cinnamon, and homemade icing (much better than canned cinnamon rolls). While some cooks wouldn't be caught using canned biscuits for anything, these rolls take only about ten minutes to prepare, and our family values that tradition as "our thing." It isn't Sunday morning at the Davises without those quick cinnamon rolls. The kids crave them when they come home for visits, and I've even been known to tote all the supplies to a freshman dorm kitchen and whip up those goodies for a freshman away at college. And so I began naming those rolls as "our tradition."

An interesting discussion starter in a group is the question "What was or is a comfort food in your family?" One group I was in offered everything from popcorn to homemade chicken noodle soup to mashed potatoes to macaroni and cheese.

A comfort food is something that you look forward to and that always makes you feel better, evokes feelings of love, or was a tradition in your family. The authors of the Comfort Foods series of cookbooks, Laurana Rayne and Norma Bannerman, say that these are foods that warm the body and soul, and connect us with special people, places, and time. "Comfort food can be hot soup on a cold day, great grandmother's biscuits warm from the oven, rice pudding for someone ill, a pot of stew for a new mother, or a thoughtfully chosen meal for friends," say Rayne and Bannerman on their website. "Meaningful connections are formed between people through preparing, serving and sharing comfort food."[1]

At one website, macaroni and cheese rated as the number-one comfort food in the United States. Chicken potpie and coleslaw rated as the second and third most favorite comfort foods. (What planet do they come from? *Coleslaw?*)

Macaroni and cheese would definitely be my youngest daughter's comfort food. I first became aware of this when she was asked to bring in and prepare her favorite family recipe for a class assignment. She chose our macaroni and cheese recipe. We had to write the recipe down for the first time.

One comfort food for many families is Friday night pizza. Ironically for many of us, carryout or delivery pizza spells home. Throwing out rules about good nutrition and eating around the table, we draw up around the television on Friday night and indulge in that wondrous greasy concoction of bread, cheese, tomato, and maybe meat. Of course, a pizza promotion council would argue that those ingredients represent the four food groups nicely. But pizza doesn't need much promotion in our society, and I'm as guilty as the next worn-out mom or dad.

Sometimes, a comforting family "home" tradition is one that many families follow on Sunday nights: everyone for himself or herself. You can fix any oddball thing you want. The kids come to like that freedom. My colleague Del Hershberger found that out when he offered to stir up a gourmet meal on a Sunday evening. His children reacted with dismay: "On Sunday night? We just want to eat whatever we want."

In our own home, Sunday night is dubbed "grab it and growl night." It is one night I don't cook, and anyone can grab whatever they want and cook or warm it up from the fridge. Don't ask me why we call it growl: I guess because Mom growls if someone fusses about having to make their own.

Sometimes all food is comfort food, and some families use food as a way to deal with conflict or depression. Have you had an argument? Eat so you feel better. And in some families, almost every meal is a "fix your own" affair, taking the specialness or comfort out of it and increasing distance between people. Too many meals are grabbed on the run and in front of the television.

While comfort foods are a wonderful part of family life and memories, overindulgence can be like Esau and his stew: too much of a good thing. We sell out our good health and the blessing of potential long life for quick satisfaction and constant poor eating habits. Consumed wisely or even sparingly, comfort foods, especially when saluted and savored as part of "our special family tradition," can be a precious way to create and cement loving family bonds.

● ● ● ● ● ● ● ● ● ●

Lasagna

Melodie Davis

When I asked my children what favorites to put in this recipe book, the first email I got back said, "You have to put in your ricotta-less lasagna recipe." This recipe makes enough for one 9x13-inch pan and a second bread pan to freeze and have handy to take to new moms or move-ins or shut-ins, or for a busy day. (Original recipe from a Better Homes and Gardens *cookbook; adapted.)*

1 pound / 500 g ground beef

1–5 cloves garlic, minced

1 tablespoon basil

1½ teaspoons salt

1 1-pound / 500 g can tomatoes, crushed or chopped

2 6-ounce / 120 g cans tomato paste

1 16-ounce / 500 g box lasagna noodles

2 eggs

3 cups / 750 ml cottage cheese

½ cup / 125 ml parmesan cheese, grated

2 tablespoons parsley flakes

1 teaspoon salt

½ teaspoon pepper

1 pound / 500 g or more mozzarella, shredded

Brown meat slowly and spoon off excess fat. Add next 5 ingredients. Simmer uncovered 30 minutes, stirring occasionally. Meanwhile, cook noodles in a large amount of boiling salted water until tender; drain and rinse. While sauce and noodles are cooking, beat the eggs, then mix the remaining ingredients together with the eggs, except for the mozzarella.

Lay two layers of noodles in a greased 9x13-inch pan. Spread with half the cottage cheese mixture. Add half the mozzarella and half the meat sauce. Repeat, saving a little mozzarella to top the lasagna. (Note: if you are making the extra bread pan on the side, save or set aside enough ingredients to put the "extra" lasagna together, roughly a quarter of each item.)

Bake immediately at 375° F / 190° C for 30 minutes. Or refrigerate or freeze before baking, in which case you'll need at least 45 minutes to bake. Cover with foil for half the baking time to save the noodles from getting dried out. (If you freeze the lasagna, it will take about a day to thaw in the refrigerator.) Let baked lasagna stand 10 minutes before cutting.

Fried Chicken

Melodie Davis

Heat ⅛ to ¼ inch of oil or shortening over medium heat. Roll chicken pieces in flour (½–1 cup). Place in hot grease. (Grease should be hot, but not smoking.)

Sprinkle chicken with salt, pepper, poultry seasoning, chili, and paprika. (Tip: mix 1 teaspoon of each in a small bowl, and take pinches from that.) Brown about 10 minutes on one side. When brown on bottom (the chicken should come up easily from the pan), turn over. Sprinkle with all seasonings again.

Cover chicken and turn heat down to low. If using bone-free pieces, ½ hour additional frying should be enough. If using chicken pieces with bones in them, fry about 40 more minutes. When done cooking, remove cover and turn up heat again to crisp up. Heat for about 5 minutes, put on paper towels, and serve.

Pizza Dough

Carmen Wyse

Saturday night is pizza night at our house. I usually make enough dough for three pizzas, which gives us supper and enough leftovers for Sunday noon and possibly lunch on Monday.

Dissolve together and set aside for about 5 minutes:
1½ cup / 375 ml warm water
2¼ teaspoons yeast

Add:
1 tablespoon oil
1 teaspoon salt

Add 4–4½ cups / 1–1.2 L flour (use as much whole wheat as you want; I often use about ⅓ cup / 75 ml). To keep the dough soft, don't add too much flour. Knead until smooth and elastic, and cover to rest 2 or more hours.

Form into 2 balls and put on floured counter. Cover and let rest at least 30 minutes. Roll out to about a 14-inch circle. Put on a pizza pan or stone.

Cover with toppings of choice (below) and bake at 450° to 500° F / 230° to 260° C for about 10 minutes. (If your pizza has just a couple of toppings, bake at the lower temperature.)

Suggestions: I bake these on pizza stones. I don't preheat my thinner stone—just sprinkle it with cornmeal and place the crust on it. I heat my thicker stone a bit when I'm preheating the oven. If it is heated too much, it makes a much crisper crust.

Chicken Pesto Pizza

Spread the dough with prepared pesto (recipe in chapter 14). Top with cooked, diced chicken and sundried tomatoes. Sprinkle parmesan and mozzarella on top, and bake as directed.

Four-Cheese Pizza

Jodi Nisly Hertzler

Sauté three to five cloves of diced garlic in a couple of tablespoons of olive oil until tender. With a pastry brush, brush the mixture onto the pizza dough. On top of this, spread ricotta cheese. Top the ricotta with slices of provolone cheese, shredded mozzarella, and shredded parmesan. Bake as directed above. Serve with marinara sauce on the side for dipping; kids love this.

Cinnamon Rolls

Rebecca Thatcher Murcia

½ cup / 125 ml milk
¼ cup / 50 ml butter
¼ cup / 50 ml water
1½ teaspoons active dry yeast
½ cup / 125 ml white sugar
½ teaspoon salt
1 egg
3 cups / 750 ml flour (can use half whole wheat)

Filling:
½ teaspoon cinnamon
½ cup / 125 ml dark brown sugar
3 tablespoons butter, softened

Warm milk and butter in a saucepan until butter melts. Remove from heat. Add water and let it cool.

In a large bowl or electric mixer, combine the milk mixture, yeast, white sugar, salt, eggs, and 1 cup flour. Mix in the remaining flour, ½ cup at a time, beating well after each addition. When the dough has pulled together, turn it onto a lightly floured surface and knead until smooth and elastic, about 8 minutes. Put dough in a lightly greased bowl and cover, and allow to rest for ½ hour.

Roll the dough out into a rectangle, approximately 12x9 inches. Spread the butter on it. In a bowl, combine the brown sugar and cinnamon, and sprinkle it over the dough. Roll up the dough, using a little water to seal the seam. Cut the roll into 12 pieces using a very sharp, serrated knife. Place in a 9x13-inch greased baking pan. (Lining the pan with parchment paper will make removing the rolls easier.) Cover and let rise until doubled, about 1 hour, or overnight in the refrigerator.

Preheat oven to 375° F / 190° C. Bake 20–25 minutes, until golden brown.

Icing:
1 cup / 250 ml powdered sugar
½ package (4 oz.) / 125 g cream cheese, softened
2 teaspoons butter, softened
¼ teaspoon vanilla
1 tablespoon milk

Combine the powdered sugar, cream cheese, and butter. Stir in the vanilla and milk. Add a little more milk, if necessary, until the frosting is a good consistency for spreading. Spread over warm cinnamon rolls.

Option: Double the cinnamon roll recipe and freeze one pan (before baking) for fresh cinnamon rolls another day.

Easy Macaroni and Cheese

Carmen Wyse and Jodi Nisly Hertzler

One of the first foods either of us thought of when working on the "comfort foods chapter" is macaroni and cheese. And to our surprise, we discovered that we both use the same recipe, which is a quick stove-top version that Alton Brown from the Food Network *developed. It comes as close to boxed mixes as we've found; it's nearly as easy and kids like it just as well. The following is Carmen's adaptation.*

1 13–16 ounce / 325–500 g package pasta, any shape
5 tablespoons butter
2 eggs
¾ cup / 175 ml milk
½ teaspoon hot sauce
1 teaspoon salt
Pepper to taste
¾ teaspoon dry mustard
2 cups / 500 ml grated sharp cheddar cheese

Cook pasta to al dente and drain. Return to the pot and melt in the butter, tossing to coat.

Whisk together the eggs, milk, hot sauce, salt, pepper, and mustard. Stir into the pasta and add the cheese. Over low heat, continue to stir for 3 minutes or until creamy.

Makes 6–8 servings.

6

• • • • • • • • •

Making Dinner Work

Given the hassle of planning a meal, getting stuff out of the freezer ahead of time, juggling the activities of children, picking up a whining toddler, being exhausted at 5:00 p.m., waiting till 8:00 p.m. for one spouse to come home, and then actually cooking a meal—do we just ditch dinner?

When I wrote my newspaper column titled "Whatever Happened to Dinner?" I asked readers to send their stories and opinions on the importance of being committed to the regular gathering of family at mealtime. I got a resounding response. The bottom line: "Hang onto dinner!"

The responses were delightful and insightful. Lisa said she and her husband began their regular family dinner tradition by placing their infant carrier on top of the dinner table. Lisa was working full time but, she said, "I still looked forward to and planned for this special time." Lisa believed if the basic habit of eating together is established from day one—before the kids can remember—it just becomes something you do every day, like going to bed.

Among those responding to my newspaper column, there was also some head-in-the-sand nostalgia for days gone by. Mabel wrote, "Those were the best days of our lives. In fact, my husband and I didn't have much time to talk at the table, [the children] furnished the conversation." Mabel remembered the days when her children walked home from school to eat lunch. (As for me, I always envied the town kids who *could* walk home for lunch. Now those *were* the days! My sister envied town kids so much she at five years old even pretended she was one by trying to walk all four miles home after school one day. A neighbor picked her up halfway home.)

A couple from Indiana wrote that having their own family business allowed them to be readily available to their children, dining together on most days. "Even then," the mother wrote, "you have to consciously decide to be available, because a family business can easily swallow up all your available time."

Jacquelyn, a longtime correspondent, said that the article about family dinner "brought such precious memories to my mind. During our four daughters' busy years in school, we still planned dinner around their commitments. It was time that we shared communally and hopefully (most of the time) appreciated each other. I was still teaching full time but found it uncommonly fulfilling to plan nutritious meals. Our girls laughingly speak of the Monday menu, the Tuesday menu."

Another parent, Ken, said he appreciated the column because it dealt more truthfully with the unpleasant sides of family meals as well—times when everyone is mad at everyone. Ken was divorced and struggling to raise two children with their mom living across the continent. "Yes, mealtime is not always great, but keep it anyway," he said.

Carolyn, a neighbor and mother of some of my kids' friends, said, "Hold out for mealtime. Even though my father wasn't home frequently at meals, we still had family mealtime, and the mealtimes I remember are the ones when he *was* there. You forget the others." Carolyn's kids learned to cook amazing meals at an early age.

Sue (name changed) and her husband disagreed about the importance of family mealtime, and reading between the lines of her email, I got the picture that he was bothered when she complained about him not helping to cook. One day he proclaimed to a friend, "I would just as soon have crackers and cheese for supper." Sue wrote, "I was a bit discouraged hearing this because . . . I have made the effort to have a nice meal on the table every night. So I thought, okay, we'll have crackers and cheese. That's what we had the first night. Then I got to thinking about my young son and what I hope to provide for him as his mother. And I thought about my favorite family memories around the dinner table. It was reassuring to know that my meals didn't have to be elaborate, but I believe gathering together needs to be a high priority. The evening meal is just one of the things that we can do to nurture the spirit of our families."

Finally in an email, Rob said,

> I too believe dinner is a lost art. In my previous life (before getting divorced) dinner was consumed in front of the television except for holidays. In my present life we try to have sit-down dinners with the television off. This was a conscious decision. My fourteen-year-old hates it. Now he has parents paying attention to his table manners. Shoving food onto the fork with a finger is the norm. Through several nights without dinner and some difficult days, I think his table manners are improving. Also, the conversation factor is a big plus. The kids have 100 percent of the parents' attention, which is difficult in these days and times. I have come to really enjoy the dinner hour and wonder how I had allowed myself to get away from it.

Rob hints at some clues to making it work: making a conscious decision and even struggling with discipline.

Steve and Leanne Benner of Harrisonburg, Virginia, wrote about their "Supper Surprise Night." When their two daughters were young, they created a long list of unusual things to do during mealtimes to insert a little fun into routine days, such as feeding each other, eating without chairs, or using pots and pans for plates.

This was how they worked it: they each wrote ideas on a small piece of paper and put the papers in a jar. Then about once a week, or whenever the mood struck, they would pull out a piece of paper and proceed with the surprise.

For this to work, they had two rules. The first was that the paper had to be drawn immediately prior to eating so that the cook couldn't cheat by making something that "fit" the situation, such as planning finger food on a "no spoon" night. The other rule was that everyone had to participate. Some of the other ideas that went into their jar included the following:

- Wear glasses.
- Everyone eat from the same large platter or tray.
- No cups (use other containers, such as canning jars).
- No talking (use gestures).
- Eat in your choice of room in the house.
- Use large utensils to eat, such as slotted spoons, spatulas, wooden spoons, dippers.
- Sing all mealtime conversation.
- Have a picnic on the floor or outside.
- Record or video the mealtime conversation, and play it back.
- Eat at a card table.
- Eat by candlelight.
- Dress in formal attire.
- Use the best china and crystal.
- Wear hats.
- Give each other new names, and call each other only those names for the meal.
- Eat dessert first.

Some of these ideas may not work at your house, but try those that you think will be enjoyed.

I still recall nights when my two sisters, my brother, and I would set up an elaborate restaurant in our kitchen and dining room. This happened only if Mom and Dad were going away for supper, and we kids were old enough to stay home by ourselves. We put up a sheet for a divider to hide the "restaurant kitchen"; created menus; appointed a waiter, cook, and diners; and usually proceeded to cook our favorite restaurant meal: hamburgers and French fries. It was a lot of work but a wonderful memory for me—though my siblings don't quite remember it. With my own kids, we had indoor picnics on a blanket in front of the television and created a pizza "hut" in the living room with a blanket over a card table.

All these ideas take cooperation and as much willingness to help with cleanup as with setup. Not every experiment has to be a roaring success. It takes parents with a certain willingness to let their hair down and to allow messes to create special family moments.

Most of these ideas require more work, not less. But sometimes the secret is being willing to relax "rules" about what constitutes a meal; this results in a whole lot *less* work. If the kids would truly like to eat only cereal for dinner, for example, why not let them do so once in a while? Except for the sugary kind, many cereals are quite nutritious. What a relief to busy parents to have "cereal night."

For me, somehow fixing breakfast for supper with pancakes and sausage or bacon was not as daunting as planning a dinner. So we would frequently have breakfast for supper and top off the meal with mixed fruit for dessert. Such a meal was always appreciated. In the summer, simply having a picnic outside is sure to be enjoyed by most.

The difference is the intentionality—deciding together that's what your family will do, rather than leaving everyone on their own to grab or fix whatever they want.

● ● ● ● ● ● ● ● ●

Jesus himself gave us a huge nudge in the direction of relaxing meal rules when he went to visit the home of his friends Mary, Martha, and Lazarus. The story is well known and found in two of the Gospels, Luke and John.

Martha was the doer and was focused on making sure she had a decent meal on the table for their friend and important guest. Mary sat at Jesus' feet, drinking in what he had to say. At the end of her patience with Mary, Martha finally flung it to Jesus: "Lord, don't you care that my sister has left me to do the work by myself? Tell her to help me."

This sisterly argument is like the script in many of our homes. "Tell her to help me!" Or the script in many marriages—one spouse getting stuck doing most of the kitchen work (let's face it, the mom more often than the dad).

Jesus offers a better way. "Martha, Martha, you are worried and upset about many things, but only one thing is needed. Mary has chosen what is better, and it will not be taken away from her" (Luke 10:41-42). If we also take this approach, it helps us make family dinnertime work in spite of the time hurdles facing us in these harried days.

● ● ● ● ● ● ● ● ● ●

One father, John, wrote to me about the inability of many in our society to take time for the "better" things. He said he didn't realize the problem was as acute as I had described. "It seems to me," he wrote, "that all our technical progress has done is to speed humans up to the speed of machines. All I can do is pray for folks to slow down and concentrate on spiritual and family concerns, with less emphasis on material things."

Pat shared this idea:

> It was always a struggle with four children and all of our assorted interests and schedules, but I thought [a gathered meal] was important for whichever ones were there, working around schedules as necessary. In the earlier years I was either at home and could fix dinner, or arrived home early enough to do it; I didn't get much help from other members of the family. But it was always my goal to have us take turns whenever possible in the preparation and cleanup. What I remember particularly, however, was reading a passage of Scripture to my daughter while she snarfed her daily breakfast bowl of boxed cereal. It took her less than two minutes. But when she appeared for breakfast, I opened the Bible and we managed to get through about two books of the New Testament in one

year, in what I hope provided a start to the day which we would look back on as having been helpful to both of us.

A two-minute breakfast *and* devotions? Hardly ideal or picture-perfect, but something this mom and daughter could do when they put their minds to it.

If you would like to establish the habit of having a meal together, perhaps you could start small, just once a week at first. As you plan for family mealtime, don't get too caught up in the common obsessions of our age: perfect kitchens, perfect homes, perfect families, perfect nutrition. Pick a meal and time that suits. Or try starting a special Saturday morning tradition of pancakes, crepes, or waffles. Some families are all at home at breakfast through the week and find that to be a better time to be together. Eat without the television or other distractions (no texting allowed, no phone calls taken), and see what happens.

I hope the ideas of other families woven into this chapter give you ways to start making dinner work. Our recipes in this chapter—some summer cookout or picnic favorites—are here to help.

●　●　●　●　●　●　●　●　●　●

Bean Burgers

Rebecca Thatcher Murcia

Note from the editors: Bean burgers are a fun alternative to hamburgers, and these grill beautifully. As a bonus, this recipe will leave you with many more beans than you need for burgers. They are beautifully seasoned, versatile, and freeze well. Consider serving leftover beans over rice as a simple main or side dish, or mash them and stir in some sour cream for a black bean dip. Or add some chicken broth and/or chopped tomatoes, and puree half for a delicious black bean soup.

8 cups / 2 L water
1 pound / 500 g black beans
2 bay leaves
1 green or red pepper, chopped
1 onion, chopped
8 cloves of garlic, chopped
2 tablespoons oregano
1 tablespoon cumin
1 tablespoon brown sugar
1½ teaspoon salt
½ teaspoon pepper
Bread crumbs or oatmeal

Let the black beans and the bay leaves simmer in 8 cups of water until they are almost soft, 45 minutes to an hour. Fry the onions, garlic, and peppers in olive oil. When the onions are translucent, add cumin and oregano, and cook for 2 more minutes. Put the onion mixture in a blender or a food processor and process briefly, then add to the bean pot. Stir in the sugar, salt, and pepper. Continue cooking over medium-low heat until the beans are soft.

Put 2 cups of the mixture in a food processor and then scrape it into a bowl. Gradually stir in bread crumbs or oatmeal until the mixture is dry enough to shape into patties.

Grill burgers until they look nicely browned, usually about 5 minutes. Flip them, put cheese on top, and cook for another 5 minutes or so. Assemble the bean burger on a toasted bun with salsa picante, lettuce, and tomatoes.

Grilled Salmon

Betty Hertzler

An often-requested dish for family birthdays.

1½ pounds / 750 g salmon fillets
⅓ cup / 75 ml soy sauce
⅓ cup / 75 ml packed brown sugar
⅓ cup / 75 ml water
¼ cup / 50 ml canola or peanut oil
3–6 garlic cloves, pressed
Lemon pepper, to taste
Salt, to taste

Combine soy sauce, brown sugar, water, oil, and garlic. Pour over fish in a zip-close plastic bag and marinate for at least 2 hours. Remove from marinade, and sprinkle with salt and lemon pepper. Grill 7 minutes on each side. If you're using a large slab of fish too unwieldy to flip on the grill, wrap it securely in aluminum foil and grill that way.

Lemon Mint Kabobs

Jodi Nisly Hertzler

This is a recipe my husband invented. Only he would have decided to do away with the process of zesting and then juicing a lemon—he tossed the whole thing into a food processor, and against my dire predictions, it worked perfectly. The mint and lemon are a wonderful summery combination. We usually make these with chicken, but the marinade could work for just about any meat.

Process together in a food processor:
1 lemon, cut in wedges
5–8 cloves of garlic
1 cup / 250 ml loosely packed mint leaves
¼ cup / 50 ml olive oil
¼ cup / 50 ml soy sauce
2 tablespoons white vinegar
2 tablespoons brown sugar
2 teaspoons salt
2 teaspoons pepper
1–2 pounds / 500–1000 g chicken or meat, cut into chunks
1 large onion, cut into wedges
2 bell peppers, any color, cut into chunks
2 lemons, cut into wedges

Marinate mixture in a zip-close plastic bag with chicken or beef, onion wedges, bell pepper chunks, and lemon wedges for 1–2 hours (or longer, if you prefer). Thread meat, veggies, and lemon wedges on skewers, and grill.

Quinoa Salad

Carmen Wyse

This is a family favorite that we adapted from a Moosewood Restaurant recipe that uses couscous instead of quinoa. I like the quinoa because it makes a good, healthy, high-protein dish.

Cover **1 cup quinoa** in a bowl with warm water, and let it soak for ½ hour. Stir well with a spoon or your fingers and then pour off water. Dump quinoa into a mesh strainer and rinse well. Put in a pan and add 1½ cup water. Bring to a boil, cover, reduce heat to low, and cook 20 minutes. Fluff with a fork. Set aside.

1 can (14 oz.) / 420 g artichoke hearts in water, cut into eighths.
½ cup / 125 ml minced scallions
2 cloves garlic, minced or pressed
1 cup / 250 ml fresh parsley, chopped
1–2 tablespoons fresh dill, chopped (1 teaspoon dried)
1 tablespoon fresh mint, chopped
3 tablespoons olive oil
Juice of ½ lemon (or more to taste)
½ cup / 125 ml toasted walnuts, chopped*
Salt and pepper to taste

Mix the artichoke hearts, scallions, garlic, and herbs into the quinoa. Stir in the oil, lemon juice, and walnuts. Add salt and pepper to taste. Serve plain or on a bed of fresh greens, chilled or at room temperature. Makes 4-6 servings.

*Hint for toasting walnuts: Pile nuts on a small plate and microwave 30 seconds, stir and do another 30 seconds. Continue until toasted.

Lemony Green Bean Salad

Jodi Nisly Hertzler

This recipe brings back memories of summer in Oregon. Our best friends there served it regularly, usually garnished with colorful, edible pansies. It was a delicious way to make use of the surfeit of beans from their garden. Perfect for a picnic or a potluck.

2–3 lbs / 1–1.5 kg fresh green beans, full length
2 lemons
1/3 cup / 75 ml canola or grape seed oil
2 cloves garlic, pressed
Salt and pepper to taste
¼ cup / 50 ml peanuts or pistachios

Steam the green beans just until they lose their squeak (5–7 minutes). Cool them in an ice-water bath and allow them to dry thoroughly in a colander lined with paper towels.

Zest and juice the lemons. Add the lemon zest (reserve approximately 1 teaspoon) and juice to a blender, and add the oil, garlic, salt, and pepper. Pour over the beans and toss. Coarsely chop the nuts, and sprinkle them and the reserved lemon zest on top.

Homemade Ice Cream

Sheri Hartzler

A birthday in our family always meant homemade ice cream. This recipe is one I found when I lived in Fort Wayne, Indiana, that has become the recipe my family uses for all birthdays—and any other time we have something to celebrate. If there is any left, it doesn't crystallize in the freezer.

1 can sweetened condensed milk
1 can evaporated milk
1 cup / 250 ml sugar
1 8-ounce / 240 ml container of Cool Whip
1 pint / 500 ml half-and-half
2 teaspoons vanilla

Put all ingredients in a 2-quart ice cream freezer. Fill to 2/3 or fill line with milk. Make ice cream according to your freezer's instructions.

7

● ● ● ● ● ● ● ● ●

So What If Dinner Isn't Picture-Perfect?

It's time to get real. As happy a childhood as I had, with its custom of a family dinner almost every night, such dinners were not all smarmy, sentimental affairs and laughter.

I remember the evening we all froze when yet another glass of water was accidentally tipped over. Dad had threatened—no, *promised*—a spanking to the person who tipped over the next glass of water at a meal. Somehow there had been a rash of tip-overs in the weeks leading up to his threat, and he surmised we were just plain careless.

Dad was not abusive, but in the fifties, most parents did not spare the rod—they spanked. I didn't get many spankings, but I do remember the sting and the humiliation.

I don't remember who got the spanking that night, but I do remember how nervous it made me: what if I were next? The very idea of a spanking hanging over your head at mealtime was so nerve-racking it produced jitters and slippery fingers. Reminiscing with my sisters recently, we all remembered Mom spilling the water once after this edict had been declared. Of course Mom did not get a spanking, and the decree quietly went away after that.

Perhaps you shudder. Perhaps you never got spanked for spilling water, but most families have mealtimes that are less than pleasant in some way. Waiting out a stubborn kid who refuses to try even one bite. Yanking a cell phone from a tween who refuses to quit receiving or sending messages to her friends. Withholding dessert because of an argument or misbehavior. Dealing with a family member who is drunk, belligerent, or mentally unstable. Watching your adolescent bolt from the table, and knowing she is going to go make herself throw up again.

When my sisters were remembering the spanking edict, one of them also pulled up a much happier memory. As Dad left the table to go watch the evening news or read the paper, he would pause, lean over Mom, wrap his arms around her from behind as she stayed seated, give her a quick peck on the cheek, and thank her for the good supper. Sometimes we were embarrassed and moaned, "Muuush," but we knew the world was a better place when both our parents were in a good mood.

Special holiday or birthday meals are occasions when we do want everyone to be on their best behavior. We strive for the Rockwellian Thanksgiving table, and while the specific dishes and customs vary between families, regions, and countries, what these occasions have in common is specific traditions and foods.

● ● ● ● ● ● ● ● ● ● ●

What do you remember about where you spent Christmas or Thanksgiving as a child? Customs vary from country to country and from place to place, but do your memories revolve around the ham or pie, your grandfather's gentle teasing, the way your grandmother smelled, or the fun you had with your cousins playing "I Spy"?

My grandparents on Dad's side lived with us, so we usually spent Thanksgiving and Christmas with my mom's family, who lived about twenty miles away. We alternated between Aunt Florence's and our house for Thanksgiving, and spent Christmas Day at my maternal grandmother's. We loved going to Aunt Florence's house because they had television and we didn't, and my cousin frequently had the latest Barbie or Barbie house or Barbie car—

all of which I never got. But the truly special thing was playing with our cousins. Blessed is the family where contacts with cousins produce happy childhood memories. The people connections are much more important than the food.

I remember differing political or theological opinions being expressed. I think almost every family has those. But I also recognized when the political or religious differences were simply glossed over or stifled. It can be wearing, frustrating, and unpleasant when you have to deal with those differences year after year.

Brenda talked about always spending Thanksgiving with an aunt who was not pleasant to be around. For this aunt, everything was always wrong with everyone else; there were frequent "organ recitals" about her ailments; and comments made to this aunt were invariably taken the wrong way. Brenda finally decided that if her own family was to have happy Thanksgiving memories, they would need to occasionally alter their Thanksgiving plans and go elsewhere for the day.

● ● ● ● ● ● ● ● ● ●

A true story from a time of international crisis helps me have a better perspective on the everyday disappointments of spilled milk and the discomforts of large family holiday meals. The story comes from the conflict in the early 1990s, in a region of the former Yugoslavia (now Bosnia and Herzegovina). The circumstances in Iraq or Afghanistan today would be similar.

During the bombing of Bosnia's capital, Sarajevo, Tamara told how after her family's second-floor apartment was destroyed by a direct hit, she, her parents, and her younger sister moved into the basement of the building. Thus began a 222-day experience they shared with twenty-two other people who'd been similarly displaced. Since most of their clothing had been destroyed, they wore the same outfits for days on end. They didn't have water, electricity, or heat—a severe hardship in Sarajevo's winter.

Tamara's parents were able to keep their jobs and were paid with two pounds of flour every two months. The only other good food they had was what they brought with them from their apartments. Tamara remembers many days of being hungry. They used furniture for firewood to cook their food.

But the occupants of that basement tried to live as normally as possible. They celebrated wedding anniversaries and birthdays. For Tamara's birthday, her parents gave her two oranges, which cost the equivalent of thirty dollars. The twenty-two people in the basement included Bosnians of Serb, Croat, and Muslim backgrounds. They tried to deal peacefully with the inevitable conflicts they had among each other.

Many of Tamara's friends died in the war, but when her sister's closest friend was killed, Tamara's parents sent her and her sister to Zagreb and on to the United States for safety. Tamara enrolled in Bucknell University and for a while spent time as an international peacemaker for the Presbyterian Peacemaking Program, from which I learned the story. She tells others how her family lived with faith in the midst of the horrors of war.

When I think about countless similar scenarios played out around the globe today, I can survive a cranky aunt's complaints or a kid's spilled water.

●   ●   ●   ●   ●   ●   ●   ●   ●   ●

Before I make everyone feel guilty for ever sitting down to a goodie-laden Thanksgiving or Christmas table, I'll echo the words of Doris Janzen Longacre in the bestselling *More-with-Less Cookbook*: "Eat with joy. In North America, the problem is more that we celebrate too often and feast nonstop."[1] Special meals and dishes for holidays and other occasions are celebrated in almost every culture, at almost every level of lifestyle. Some people sacrifice greatly—even to the point of going into debt—to prepare food for week-long, community-wide celebrations such as weddings. We would do well to tap into this tradition of extending our tables to include the forgotten and the unlovely at holiday times, making sure "the whole village" is fed.

According to the Gospels, Jesus participated in wedding parties and other feasts. His penchant for shaking up the religious establishment by eating with outcasts and "sinners" is revealed when he quotes what others say about him: "Here is a glutton and a drunkard, a friend of tax collectors and 'sinners'" (Matthew 11:19). In Luke he's shown eating with the hated, cheating tax collector, Zacchaeus (see Luke 19:1-10). So Jesus was not a stranger to gathered mealtimes where conflict brewed and religious differences were muffled for the day.

Thus Jesus himself gives us an important lesson to remember in raising our families, especially through holiday times. Appearances or a picture-perfect meal is not the goal; rather, we should strive to open ourselves to others, even those with whom we don't always mix. As you plan your special-occasion meals and holiday celebrations with families, think about those left out of such celebrations, and mix up the table a bit.

● ● ● ● ● ● ● ● ● ●

Christmas Morning French Toast

Jodi Nisly Hertzler

This dish is a specialty of a bed and breakfast that my husband and I visited when we lived in Oregon. We returned the following year, and I requested the same dish—it was that good. Rich and decadent, it's perfect for a holiday brunch. Even better, it's deceptively simple, and all the preparation is done the evening before, so all you have to do is pop it in the oven the next morning. I strongly recommend using challah in this dish, if you can find it.

1 stick (½ cup) unsalted butter
1 cup / 250 ml packed brown sugar
2 tablespoons corn syrup
1 cup / 250 ml pecans, chopped fairly fine
½ cup / 125 ml dried cranberries
½ large Granny Smith apple, diced
1 loaf French bread, challah, baguette, or round country-style bread
5 large eggs
1½ cup / 375 ml half-and-half
2 teaspoons vanilla
¼ teaspoon salt

In a small, heavy saucepan, melt butter with brown sugar and corn syrup over moderate heat, stirring until smooth. Add the nuts, cranberries, and apples, and stir to coat. Pour into a 9x13 baking dish.

Cut ½-inch thick slices of bread and arrange them in one layer in the baking dish, squeezing them slightly to fit. (Alternatively, divide everything into 6 separate ramekins—small ceramic or glass serving bowls—and bake individual servings.)

In a bowl, whisk together the eggs, half-and-half, vanilla, and salt until well combined, and pour evenly over the bread. Refrigerate at least 8 hours and up to one day.

Preheat oven to 350° F / 180° C and bring bread to room temperature. Bake uncovered, in middle of oven until puffed and edges are golden, 35–40 minutes. Makes 6–8 servings.

Option: Leave out the nuts and fruit for a simpler dish—that's how it was originally served to me.

Easy Cranberry Salad

Melodie Davis

My mother and grandmother's recipe and process for cranberry salad was long and complicated. After purchasing expensive cranberry salad from delis for several years to satisfy my cravings, I got this much easier recipe from a church friend, Alisa Hillary.

1 small box orange gelatin dessert
1 can whole cranberries in sauce
1 cup / 250 ml chopped celery
¾ cup / 175 ml chopped nuts (pecan or walnut)
1 cup / 250 ml chopped apple pieces
1 cup / 250 ml chopped orange pieces

Make orange gelatin according to package instructions, but use only 1 cup water to dissolve. Mix all together. Let jell in refrigerator 3–4 hours.

Shrimp Creole

Betty Hertzler

This has become a mainstay of our family's Christmas dinner. It's delicious and festive, but easy enough for a weeknight meal. It can be made in advance and gently reheated on the stove.

½ cup / 125 ml chopped onion
½ cup / 125 ml chopped celery
1–3 cloves garlic, minced
3 tablespoons olive oil
1 16-ounce / 500 g can tomatoes
1 8-ounce / 240 g can tomato sauce
1½ teaspoons salt
1 teaspoon sugar
1 tablespoon Worcestershire sauce
½ to 1 teaspoon chili powder
Dash hot pepper sauce
2 teaspoons cornstarch
1 pound / 500 g frozen shelled shrimp, thawed
½ cup / 125 ml chopped green pepper

In a skillet, cook onion, celery, and garlic in oil until tender but not brown. Add tomatoes, tomato sauce, salt, sugar, Worcestershire sauce, chili powder, and hot pepper sauce. Simmer uncovered 45 minutes. Mix cornstarch with 1 tablespoon cold water; stir into sauce. Cook and stir until thickened and bubbly. Add shrimp and green pepper. Cover. Simmer 5 minutes. Serve over rice.

Spinach Mashed Potatoes

Carmen Wyse

Wayne's mother makes this for every holiday dinner. She often makes it up the day before the big meal, keeps it refrigerated, and then pulls it out the day of the meal and bakes (may take a bit longer to bake if it goes into the oven cold).

6–8 large potatoes
¾ cup / 175 ml yogurt or sour cream
1 stick butter
2 teaspoons salt
¼ teaspoon pepper
1 cup / 250 ml shredded cheddar cheese
2 tablespoons chopped chives
¼ teaspoon dried dill weed
2 pounds / 1 kg frozen chopped spinach

Cook and mash potatoes. Cook spinach in microwave for 2–3 minutes or until thawed and warm. Squeeze out water.

To the potatoes, add sour cream or yogurt, butter, salt, and pepper. Beat until light and fluffy. Add chives, dill, and spinach. Place in 2–3 quart casserole and top with cheese. Bake at 400° F / 200° C for 20 minutes.

Sweet Potato Delight

Burton Buller

For every family Christmas and Thanksgiving feast, we could be sure that Mother would serve sweet potatoes topped with marshmallows. When I was a child, it was one of my favorites. In Virginia, we discovered another sweet potato recipe that we've modified a bit, and it has now become the sweet potato dish of choice for our own family feasts. It is a very popular dish for church potlucks. Never any left over! Make this ahead of time and refrigerate overnight, to bake the next day. It is also yummy reheated.

4 cups / 1 L baked sweet potatoes, peeled and mashed
⅓ cup / 75 ml melted butter
2 beaten eggs
1 cup / 250 ml milk
2 teaspoons vanilla extract
⅔ cup / 150 ml sugar
½ cup / 125 ml chopped pecans or walnuts
½ cup / 125 ml shredded coconut

Topping:
½ cup / 125 ml chopped pecans or walnuts
½ cup / 125 ml shredded coconut
3 tablespoons butter, melted

(Note: This recipe is for sweet potatoes that have been baked or microwaved. If using boiled sweet potatoes, reduce milk to ½ cup. If you find the dish too dry after baking, add ½ cup / 125 ml milk. I've found that the moisture content of the sweet potatoes significantly alters the final texture.)

Preheat oven to 375° F / 190° C. Combine sweet potatoes, butter, eggs, milk, vanilla extract, sugar, nuts, and coconut in a large mixing bowl. Spread the mixture into a greased 1½ quart / 1.5 L casserole dish.

Combine the topping ingredients, then sprinkle over the sweet potato mixture. Bake for 25 minutes.

Candied Nuts

Carmen Wyse

When I was growing up, my mother made these for holidays, often using peanuts. I now make them every Christmas to give as gifts to school teachers or Sunday school teachers. But my family is sad if I don't keep some for us to eat.

1 cup / 250 ml sugar
½ cup / 125 ml water
1 teaspoon salt
1 pound / 500 g nuts (I like pecans)
1 teaspoon vanilla
½ teaspoon cinnamon

Mix sugar, salt, and water in a large pan. Bring to a simmer over medium heat and cook 5 minutes, stirring frequently. Add the nuts and cook, continuing to stir until they start looking sugary and whitish. Add vanilla and cinnamon, and cook and stir a bit more until nuts are sugary and loose in the pan (should not be sticky). Pour out onto waxed paper and cool.

Davis Apple Pie

Melodie Davis

The old song goes, "Can she bake a cherry pie?" which stereotypically tested a potential sweetheart's viability as a mate. For me, it was the apple pie test. I made an apple pie that my fiancé loved so much he asked me to go to his father's home (a widower) and make a bunch of apple pies. This recipe became part of our Davis lore, but it is pretty ordinary. The key is ample cinnamon, and the types of apples you use; we like Stayman the best, but any tart apple is good.

Crust (for a 2-crust 9-inch pie):
2 cups / 500 ml flour
1 teaspoon salt
⅔ cup / 150 ml shortening plus 2 tablespoons
¼ cup / 50 ml water

Mix flour and salt, then cut in shortening. When shortening and flour are mixed to make clumps the size of peas, add water. Mix by hand until a clump of dough forms. Divide into two balls. Roll out bottom crust for pie pan on a well-floured board with a floured rolling pin. Carefully lift with a turner and put in pan. Roll out second pie crust for top, slicing a few decorative holes with knife to allow steam to escape. Leave crust to rest on your board until you fill the pie the with apple mixture.

Apple mixture:
5 cups / 1.3 L peeled and sliced tart apples
1 cup / 250 ml sugar
1 tablespoon flour
¼ teaspoon salt
1 teaspoon cinnamon
1 teaspoon lemon juice

Mix apples and all ingredients in a bowl, then put it in the crust. Pat edge of crust with water to help bottom and top crust to seal. Put on top crust, and pinch together, pressing with fork or your own pattern of twists. Protect crust from getting overly brown by using foil around edge of pie pan. Bake in a 425° F / 220° C oven for 10 minutes, then lower heat to 350° to 375° F / 180° to 190° C for another 50 minutes. Remove from oven and let cool.

8

• • • • • • • • •

Eat My Grits!
The Kitchen Culture Wars

Did you ever fix a wonderful dish that was a traditional favorite when you were growing up and serve it to your spouse or spouse's family?

When I was first married and served some of my family's favorites to my new husband, I would ask how he liked them. Mostly Stuart loved my cooking, but sometimes he would respond, "Er, you don't have to make that again."

It was then that I felt like reeling off a line from an old television show, *Alice*, with a gum-chewing, hardscrabble waitress, Flo, sparring frequently with the owner of the diner, Mel. When Mel or a customer would tick off Flo, her signature retort was, "Well kiss mah grits!" (each word pronounced with a long southern drawl).

One of my family's holiday traditions was cranberry salad. I'm not talking about a can of congealed cranberry sauce here. I'm talking about a recipe that is so hard to make, I had to replace it with a much easier one (described in the previous chapter). For my mother and grandmother, cranberry salad was a production of a couple of hours, in which you ground the cranberries, grated orange peel (zest), ground the nuts, and cut up oranges. This was in the days before food processors made such an operation a flick of a button. One of my favorite childhood Thanksgiving chores was putting together the metal grinder with all its parts and churning out those ground cranberries.

One year as a fairly new bride, I was really hungry for cranberry salad and spent hours on the dish for my husband's family for Thanksgiving, only to have it receive polite nibbles. I learned it wasn't a traditional favorite for that family. (Now several sons-in-law have joined the family who do enjoy a small serving of cranberry salad.)

The culture of cooking and sharing in families and what we like or don't like fascinates me. As a young, immature bride, I felt threatened and disappointed to have food passed over or rejected, but I now enjoy dissecting regional and family differences. In the South, you have almost a whole different culture from that in the North in regard to cooking—or maybe five or six different cultures. When I moved from Indiana to the deep South, I learned about fried okra, black-eyed peas, grits, and *real* iced tea (always brewed, always sweetened while still hot). In Kentucky, I learned about shucky beans and collard or turnip greens. I know Louisiana has a different batch of regional favorites. Spritzing malt vinegar on French fries, as the Canadians do, seems strange for those of us who live south of that border.

My husband's Aunt Mary of Montgomery, Alabama, visited us and made several "old favorites" for her brother, my husband's father. One item was a coconut cake with fresh coconut that you grated yourself. The cake took four hours to make—and that's why you won't find it in this collection. Her coconut frosting melted in our mouths like cotton candy, and there was not a piece of the four-layer delicacy left by the end of the meal. "People don't cook like this anymore," Aunt Mary observed.

For many Southerners, grits are a breakfast staple. *Grits*, to the uninitiated, may sound awful—like eating dirt, I suppose. When our family was in Richmond, Virginia, eating breakfast at a hotel's complimentary buffet, a college women's athletic team from Maine was also going through the line. One of the athletes turned to me and asked, "Can you tell me whether this white stuff is cream of wheat, or what?"

Smiling, I answered, "No, those are grits!" The girl actually grimaced. "You are in the South," I added gently.

I used to be clueless as well, growing up in "Yankee" Indiana. My first introduction to grits came at a Mennonite church youth convention near Asheville, North Carolina. All of us northern kids groused at first about the white, gooey stuff on our breakfast plates every morning. But I learned that grits are rather tasty with a pat of butter and salt and pepper. Other people like grits with maple syrup or honey.

Grits come from hominy—what's left from a kernel of corn after the yellow "cap" has been taken off. The dictionary describes grits as ground hominy with the germ removed. They are low in fat and sodium but have a decent amount of iron, all for only pennies a serving—a cheap and filling breakfast that sticks to your ribs. Grits can be eaten by people with allergies to wheat flour. Cheese grits is a variation on the basic dish and can be served as a meat substitute. My pastor for many years, Ann Held, almost always brought her cheese grits to our church potlucks, something many of us greatly anticipated (see the recipe in this chapter).

• • • • • • • • • • •

I soon learned to avoid disappointment during holidays by recognizing the fundamental difference between families and all the food cultures that exist. Don't expect that a dish you loved when growing up can be made to taste exactly the same as "mother used to make." Don't expect that a different family will greet your tradition eagerly. My mother loved having oyster soup on Christmas Eve, because it was a tradition her family observed. None of my brothers and sisters were big fans of oyster soup (except for the little oyster crackers), so eventually she gave up that tradition and for some years enjoyed cooking hot dogs in the fireplace on Christmas Eve.

Sometimes new family favorites grow on us. I now love Virginia country ham and fried oysters. And if you aren't quite sure what Virginia country ham is, it's the super-salty stuff that can be a delicacy like prosciutto when sliced thin and eaten in little biscuits. To which a real Virginian like my husband would scoff and say, "Nah, the real way to eat country ham is fried thick and put in a sandwich."

I still love my mother's green beans, cooked and then blackened lightly in a cast-iron skillet, but I also love the Davis green beans, which simmer for hours on a stove with a light touch of country ham—all nutrition long gone, but tasty in a different way.

The first time I faced black-eyed peas in my school cafeteria in northern Florida, I thought they looked like mushy baby rats. Now I love them—when I get a chance to eat them (although I don't cook them for myself).

● ● ● ● ● ● ● ● ● ●

I subtitled this chapter "The Kitchen Culture Wars," but did you know that a woman in the Bible once prepared a meal that actually prevented a war, or at least what was certain to have been a fierce and deadly battle? Abigail was the "intelligent and beautiful" wife of Nabal, who was wealthy but "surly and mean" (1 Samuel 25:3). Once, when David and his men were fleeing from King Saul and his men, David heard that Nabal and his servants were nearby shearing sheep. He sent an entourage seeking supplies for his camp, with a message reminding Nabal that David's men had been friendly, never robbing from Nabal's men and treating them well.

Nabal's response *was* "surly and mean" (just like the Bible described him, and it adds that his name means "fool.") "Who is this David?" the NIV phrases his response. "Why should I take my [supplies], and give it to men coming from who knows where?" (v. 10-11)

Them's fightin' words, so when David heard about Nabal's response, he told his guys, "Put on your swords!" One of Nabal's servants got wind of the brewing fight and told Abigail about it, filling in how David's men had been good to Nabal's and how they had even formed a human wall of protection around their sheep camp.

"Now think it over and see what you can do," the servant told Abigail, "because disaster is hanging over our master and his whole household. He is such a wicked man that no one can talk to him" (v. 17). Meanwhile, David was calling on God to deal harshly with him if he and his men left one male alive in Nabal's camp.

Abigail took bread, wine, lamb, grain, raisin and fig cakes and, without telling Nabal, went with a party to meet David. Abigail and her peace meal did the trick, and David's men didn't pursue their plan. When Abigail returned home, Nabal was holding his own banquet and was quite drunk. She waited until his hangover cleared and told him how she had saved their household from certain death. "His heart failed him," the Bible reports (v. 37). Nabal died ten days later. And David, never one to let a pretty woman slip away, promptly married Abigail.

The point of using this story here? Food and hospitality, rather than engendering kitchen wars and irritation in families, can help bridge divides, cultural and otherwise, between people.

In Abigail's day, I'm sure that cooking the amount of food she prepared for David's camp was a community affair, many household hands making light work. In our part of the country, if you have a reason to be on the road at the unrighteous hour of four on a Saturday morning, you can witness the same thing. Through spring, summer, and most of the fall, you may see smoke rising from a pole barn or shelter behind a church or community building, as if some strange ritual were taking place. You may see lanterns or lights in the predawn hours and a small cadre of people working, drinking coffee, keeping warm.

What's going on? A chicken barbecue, of course. Early-morning activities like this take place in most communities in North America. Whether it is the local Lions Club rising to prepare their annual pancake and sausage breakfast, the Music Boosters making homemade soup for the fall festival, the volunteer firefighters preparing their turkey-and-oyster supper, or various stripes of Mennonites holding a massive relief sale—working together in clubs, church, and community organizations to raise funds is part of our food tradition. These groups frequently work to raise money for causes ranging from scholarships to famine relief to vision and hearing screening to athletic teams for local youngsters.

But I'm not sure the funds raised are as important as something else that happens. These are the local traditions that mean home, family, community, faith, fond memories. They are about working together, especially when you are working across generations. They are a way to teach faith and values to children.

What happens as you work with others to prepare vast amounts of great food? You get to know each other in new and deeper ways, even if the learning is not always pleasant. You learn who makes a good supervisor and who is just plain bossy.

You learn each others' comfort levels based on the ratio of the quantity of food prepared to the expected rush of customers. "Isn't it time to put some more sausages on?" asks Joe, eyeing the kettle of finished sausages that is still adequate but diminishing.

"Nah, I'll wait till I see a few more people in line," responds Jim. "I want 'em to be good and fresh."

You learn who can really hustle and who mostly likes to stand around. You learn who can see work to be done and who has to be told every time the chicken needs turning. Working together is the best way to get to know other people in your club or organization, and the same is true in a church. The way to feel more at home is to get involved, to take on a job or committee assignment and help out behind the scenes.

These are the kinds of events that bind whole communities together, creating special memories for children and families. They are part of what make home, home. At a pancake breakfast, when I was working with my Lion husband, I was surprised to see a group of high school and college kids show up to eat at about 7:45 a.m., when most teens aren't even thinking about rolling out of bed on a Saturday morning. One of them exclaimed, "Oh, I couldn't miss the Lions pancake breakfast. This is just part of our tradition. Our family did it every year."

So when you see smoke rising or homemade posters announcing a local event, think: this is not just about somebody's fundraiser. This is not just about our favorite local specialty. This is about family and community.

People, clans, and tribes have been coming together around food for centuries. When a child or a colleague is standing over your shoulder, either critiquing or eager to learn a new cooking skill, and you'd really rather just do it your way or do it yourself, just keep in mind the value of "community" cooking.

I've enjoyed getting recipes for dishes or treats prepared at community fundraisers and then cooking them at home. This chapter includes a few such dishes, along with some favorite foods for potluck meals.

● ● ● ● ● ● ● ● ● ●

Sheri's Chocolate Cake

Sheri Hartzler

This recipe came from a friend originally and quickly became the family favorite whenever we wanted chocolate cake. Quick and easy to make. Putting it in a large sheet pan instead of a regular-size cake pan makes it a great dessert for a church potluck.

Sift together:

3 cups / 750 ml flour

2 cups / 500 ml sugar

⅓ cup / 75 ml cocoa

2 teaspoons baking soda

½ teaspoon salt

Add to dry ingredients (don't overmix):

2 cups / 500 ml water

⅔ cup / 150 ml melted shortening or butter

2 tablespoons vinegar

1 teaspoon vanilla

Bake at 350° F / 180° C in two 9-inch round pans or one 12-inch by 17-inch sheet cake pan for 25–30 minutes.

Chocolate Cake Frosting

⅓ cup / 75 ml soft butter or margarine
⅓ cup / 75 ml cocoa
2 cups / 500 ml powdered sugar
1½ teaspoon vanilla
About 2 tablespoons milk

Mix butter and cocoa. Blend in sugar. Stir in vanilla and milk. Beat until smooth.

Sheri's chocolate cake is tasty, quick, and versatile, so we thought it would be fun to provide recipes for a couple of icings, if you feel like trying something a little different. Both of the following come from the collection of Carmen Wyse.

Fluffy White Icing

5 tablespoons flour
1 cup / 250 ml milk
1 stick butter, softened
½ cup / 125 ml shortening
1 cup / 250 ml sugar
½ teaspoon vanilla

Mix the flour and milk together, and cook until very thick. Cool. Cream the shortening, butter, flour, and vanilla together. Add flour/milk mixture and beat at least 5 minutes or until smooth and silky.

Variation: For chocolate icing, add about 1/3 cup / 75 ml cocoa powder to the flour/milk mixture.

Easy Penuche Icing

My aunt brought a chocolate cake with this icing to a family reunion. My husband Wayne was thrilled, made a huge fuss over it, and asked for the recipe. We received it in the mail a short time later. The whole family now knows that if there is chocolate cake, Wayne is going to ask for penuche icing. It really is good—and it is just fun to say penuche!

½ cup / 125 ml butter
1 cup / 250 ml brown sugar
¼ cup / 50 ml milk
1¾ cup / 425 ml powdered sugar

Melt butter, add brown sugar, and boil 2 minutes, stirring constantly. Add milk and bring back to a boil. Remove from heat and cool to lukewarm. Add powdered sugar a little at a time, beating until it is nice and creamy. Spread on cake.

Brunswick Stew

Melodie Davis

G. Don Whitmore, feed salesman, treasurer, and all-around elder for our congregation, introduced my family to this Virginia favorite. He would make large quantities for our congregational meeting potlucks or other church events. This recipe (my adaptation) comes from the collection of another Virginia cook, Martha Doughtie Cavanaugh, in Gather Round Our Table: A Southern Family Shares Recipes and Memories from the Doughtie Family and Friends *(compiled by Edith Vick Farris, 2005, G & R Publishing).*

1 4-pound / 2 kg whole chicken or 3 large frozen boneless/
      skinless breasts
1 14-ounce / 420 g package frozen baby lima beans
1 10-ounce / 300 g package or can of corn
1 quart / 1 L diced tomatoes
1 egg, beaten
6 white potatoes, peeled and diced
1 sleeve saltine crackers, crushed
Lots of pepper (to taste)
Salt to taste
Pieces of ham seasoning (cooked ham bone, ham hock)

Cover chicken with water and cook for one hour (if using chicken breasts, replacing some of the water with chicken stock gives it more flavor). If using whole chicken, strain out the fat, then pull out the bones. Dice or shred all meat and return it to the broth. If using breasts, the meat will come apart during further cooking and stirring. Do not pour out broth.

Add all remaining ingredients, cover, and simmer for 2–3 hours, stirring occasionally to avoid sticking. Or put the stew into a slow cooker and cook for 8–10 hours on low. Serve immediately, or refrigerate and gently reheat when you're ready to serve (this tastes better).

Chicken BBQ

Melodie Davis

We got this vinegar-based sauce from my father, Vernon Miller, who was known for his BBQ chicken in northern Indiana (among our church and family friends, anyway); his recipe came from the Farm Bureau. However, in these parts of Virginia, they claim it as a Virginia recipe, and a variation of this is used everywhere, including at the Virginia Mennonite Relief Sale. In the proportions I have below, this is a nice amount for a cookout for family or company and will cover 5–6 chicken halves or 10–12 boneless chicken breasts or pieces. It can be easily multiplied for larger groups.

Mix together:
1 cup / 250 ml vinegar
1 cup / 250 ml water
½ cup / 125 ml butter or margarine, melted
¼ cup 50 ml Worcestershire sauce
¼ cup / 50 ml salt
½ teaspoon pepper
Add other seasoning(s) as desired:
½ teaspoon chili
½ teaspoon garlic powder
Dash sugar or honey
Dry mustard

Marinate ahead of time or just douse chicken frequently as you grill: 2–3 hours for chicken halves, 30–35 minutes for chicken tenders. Turn chicken halves about every 15 minutes.

Reserve some sauce to steam finished meat with when you take it off the fire; put it into a 5-quart Dutch oven and pour a small amount of "clean" sauce (some that has not encountered raw meat) over the chicken. Keep warm until served, or steam for 5–10 minutes.

Cheese Grits Casserole

Melodie Davis

This is a standard dish at almost all potlucks at my church, contributed by our pastor, Ann Held. Ann will be quick to tell you she's not a cook, but this dish always disappears fast.

Preheat the oven to 350° F / 180° C. Boil 6 cups / 1.5 L of water. Add 1½ cup / 375 ml quick-cooking grits. Bring to a boil, then lower flame and cook until water is absorbed.

Stir in:

1 stick butter or margarine
1 pound / 500 g grated sharp cheddar cheese
3 eggs, beaten lightly
2 teaspoons Lawry seasoning salt
5–6 drops Tabasco sauce

Pour into a greased 9x13-inch baking dish. Bake 1 hour. Let stand 10 minutes before serving.

Suggestions: These are great served alongside the Barbeque Spareribs or Pork Chops in chapter 3 or the Chicken BBQ in this chapter. Or try them with some spicy Cajun or steamed shrimp.

Shrimp Rice Salad

Betty Hertzler

A friend of mine brought this to a gathering, and it was so good I had to get the recipe from her. It's good alone or served on a bed of greens, or even eaten on crackers.

1¾ cup / 425 ml mayonnaise
3 tablespoons lemon juice
Dash of Tabasco sauce
Salt to taste
4 green onions, sliced
½ cup / 125 ml chopped celery
½ cup / 125 ml sliced stuffed olives
1 cup / 250 ml cauliflower florets, chopped
½ cup / 125 ml red or green pepper, chopped
10–12 ounces / 300–360 g salad shrimp
Fresh parsley for garnish (optional)
Sprinkle of paprika for garnish (optional)

Cook 1 cup / 250 ml long grain white rice (yields about 3 cups / 750 ml cooked), and set aside to cool. Combine the mayonnaise, lemon juice, Tabasco sauce, and salt in a small bowl. Set aside. Combine the chopped vegetables, then stir in the cooled rice.

Pour the dressing over the salad, and stir to coat. Fold in the shrimp, and refrigerate overnight. Garnish with a sprinkle of paprika and fresh chopped parsley before serving, if you wish.

Funnel Cakes

Melodie Davis

This lawn party or fairgrounds food is easier than you might expect to make at home. We began many a holiday morning with it—not Christmas or Easter, but the lazy summer holiday mornings when no one has to go to work: Memorial Day, July 4, or Labor Day. You need a funnel to make this spiral-shaped quick bread.

2 eggs, beaten
1½ cup / 375 ml milk
2 cups / 500 ml sifted flour
1 teaspoon baking powder
½ teaspoon salt
2 cups / 500 ml cooking oil
1 cup / 250 ml confectioner's sugar (for topping)

In mixing bowl, combine eggs and milk, and set aside. Sift together flour, baking powder, and salt. Add to egg mixture. Beat smooth with egg beater or whisk. Test to see if it flows easily through a funnel; if too thick, add milk; too thin, add flour.

In 8- or 9-inch skillet, heat cooking oil to 360° F / 180° C. Cover the bottom opening of the funnel with a finger, and pour a generous half-cup of batter into the funnel. (Keep children back—it can splatter hot grease.) Hold funnel close to oil and release batter in a spiral shape. Fry until golden, about 3 minutes. Turn cake carefully, using tongs and a spatula. Cook 1 minute more. Drain on paper towel.

Move to a serving plate and sift confectioner's sugar or cinnamon on top. Best eaten fresh as they come off the stove.

9

• • • • • • • • •

Snowball Cake, Coffee Cookies, and Other Cooking Disasters

My youngest daughter was about nine when she got in the mood one day for one of her favorite cookies, which we call Snowball Cookies, a rich shortbread-cookie I usually make at Christmas (some people call them Russian Tea Cakes). So Doreen decided to make them herself.

I had to leave the house while she was stirring them up. You guessed it; we had one of those cooking disasters that happen frequently when a child is learning something new.

Instead of a teaspoon of water, she put in a cup. Instead of a stiff dough ball, she had runny batter.

So, echoing the quote often attributed to Marie Antoinette, I proclaimed, "Let them eat cake!" I added eggs and we baked it, and sure enough, it turned out to be an edible cake.

I shared the cake at the office—office people are always suckers for any baking disaster—and my colleagues told about other cooking disasters they had experienced in their families.

One remembered a child who put two tablespoons of pepper in a chicken dish instead of one teaspoon.

Another woman's sister fixed a wonderful dish of baked chicken thighs. Only she baked it way too long, and the family now enjoys recalling the dry, shriveled little thighs they tried to consume that night.

The child of another colleague decided to make pancakes for her family, using a box mix. Since she knew that to make a cake you use an entire box, she used the *entire box* of pancake mix for their family of five.

And our family still jokes about the coffee cookies my sister made. The recipe called for "one cup of coffee." She put in a whole cup of coffee granules. The recipe, of course, meant liquid coffee, already brewed. The cookies were not only bitter, they were so hard the dog wouldn't eat them.

Such are the stories family lore is made of. You never live them down. You will always be known as the one who ruined canned spaghetti and meatballs by adding a cup of water.

"I can't figure out why kids aren't learning how to cook," a man told me one day. He and his wife don't have any children, and he was talking about the college-age kids he worked with. Kids aren't learning how to cook because we don't have the time to teach them. When evening meals are prepared and eaten in a forty-five-minute gap between the end of basketball practice and the time to leave for piano lessons, how can you include teaching kids to cook? My one sister never learned to cook as a kid because she was the one who gravitated more naturally to farm work; she was usually in the barn when it came time to hang out in the kitchen, observing cooking in progress.

It is hard to find time, but I think it is valuable to try to teach kids to cook anyway, in whatever snatches of time you do find, even if it is only to make egg sandwiches.

Take the scenario of having only forty-five minutes between basketball and piano lessons. In the thirty minutes you have at home, you let your son break and turn the eggs while you throw plates, juice, and applesauce on the table. Even if you have only ten minutes to sit down as a family, at least you have that much time together.

Then when your son moves to an apartment at some point, at least that is one burger meal he won't have to buy out. But my guess is that once kids start cooking, they'll want to expand their menu by learning to cook other things. When my kids were in this busy-but-learning-to-cook stage, we slowly added menus and recipes to a loose-leaf binder. The kids were on tap to cook when I was out of town on business, and eventually we had enough options for almost a week of their cooking.

I'm happy to report that Doreen's next baking project at the age of nine, after the cookie-turned-cake near-disaster, were two of the prettiest loaves of bread you ever saw or ate (see Doreen's Oatmeal Bread in chapter 1). She can still turn out better-looking loaves than I can, because she takes more time with them than her slap-dash, always-in-a-hurry mom. She was the one who, as a child, cooked things for the county fair and won ribbons.

I was driving our oldest daughter and my neighbor's twelve-year-old son to their band concert one rushed evening when they both had to be there early for warm-up. The boy casually commented that he had made supper, since his mother was sick.

I figured Greg had thrown some hot dogs in the microwave or fixed some soup. But no. He had prepared herb chicken, baked potatoes, cut up and cooked fresh broccoli. Plus he cleaned some vegetables to eat with dip. For a family of six.

Frankly, I was in shock, and felt more than a little guilty. I thought my daughters were doing pretty well, but they couldn't have come close to producing a meal like that. So I asked his mother, Carolyn Sachs, how she managed so well. Carolyn and her husband, Steve, had four children and at the time of this story, the kids were ages four through twelve. Carolyn was home full time but taught piano lessons from her home studio.

"It started when our third child was born," Carolyn said. The older children had always enjoyed helping in the kitchen by doing things like shaping their own lump of bread dough into a little loaf. But with Carolyn's life suddenly busier than ever, she began letting the older two, Greg and Martha, ages six and five, have more responsibility. "I'd say, 'Martha, why don't you make a fruit salad for dinner,' and give her some suggestions for what she could include. But then she would decide what actually went in."

The next step in their progress was learning to cut things up. "You start with soft things they can easily cut on a cutting board. They first cut mushrooms, zucchini, and bananas."

Carolyn says she trained herself to "look the other way" unless needed. That is the hard part. But she had a slight advantage in that, by working out of her home, she was present in case of emergency, although not readily available to be bothered for every little need. A babysitter also supervised the children on some days.

Carolyn said her children soon wanted to be responsible for making whatever items they needed for school parties. When Martha was eleven, she made crescent rolls for a French class party. By age twelve, Greg was making cookies and had made simple pies.

"Sometimes I'll look in, observe the way they're going about a job, and say something like, 'When I measure shortening, I find it easiest to do it this way,'" explained Carolyn. After all, she is a professional teacher who taught my second daughter, Tanya, piano from age eight through eighteen.

The Sachs children were also responsible to clean up after they cooked, which is hard to get children—and even adults—to do. "We started by working on cleanup together," Carolyn said, but by early adolescence, they were expected to do it themselves.

Carolyn mentioned reading an article about a mom who watched her friend jumping up to serve her children's needs at every turn. The author felt that while that spirit of service may be beautiful, it is much better in the long run to equip children to be independent. I had a lot to learn in that department too.

Sometimes kids don't learn to cook because their parents don't want the mess or set standards too high. A seventy-year-old woman told me sadly that her mother never wanted her in the kitchen. Her mom was a neatnik and didn't want to take the time to involve her daughter. While we can understand not having time and not wanting flour all over the kitchen, the kitchen can offer a priceless training ground and space for togetherness between parent and child. Even washing dishes goes much better when one person is preparing dishes for the washer and the other is loading.

Kids are masters at learning that if they claim to be working on homework, they can wiggle out of helping with dinner or cleanup. But they can also learn to manage their time to include chores. Sometimes I had to remind our daughters that I had other work to do, too, and I just have to get up earlier or not spend as much time with television to get my housework and office work done. It's the same way for them. Children can learn good time-management skills by needing to squeeze time for cooking between homework and hanging out.

In spite of our culture's busyness, cooking has enjoyed a renaissance of popularity. The Food Channel provides cooking classes that fill the void for people who did not learn basic cooking skills growing up. My oldest daughter, the one who mistakenly added water to spaghetti and meatballs, now knows how to make crème brûlée and fixes some tasty fresh scallops—two things I've never even tried to make. As a young adult, she took a gourmet cooking class for several months and enjoyed herself immensely. It also increased her confidence to branch out and try making many new recipes that were not covered in class.

● ● ● ● ● ● ● ● ● ●

One of the best food stories in the Bible has to be the "manna" experience of the children of Israel (Exodus 16)—a story that is referred to throughout the Bible. After leaving Egypt, the Israelites are living in the desert and complaining because they miss the meat and other goodies they enjoyed when they lived in captivity in Egypt. When Moses takes the complaint to the Lord, God provides quail and manna for them every day, except the Sabbath; they are to save a double measure the day before. The miraculous appearance of the white sweet bread that "tasted like wafers made with honey" keeps the Israelites from starving (v. 31).

For children who don't learn to cook, there ain't gonna be no manna making a miraculous appearance for them every day, and most of them won't have Mom or Dad providing for them either. They will have three options: (1) pray for a spouse who knows how and loves to cook; (2) eat out all the time; or (3) eat cereal or canned spaghetti and meatballs every day for the rest of their lives. Not fun or realistic. Keeping dinner in families—and providing at least some basic cooking opportunities—is part of how we help our children grow up.

Letting very young kids help cook their favorite food gets them started on a lifelong love affair with cooking (we hope). Three-year-olds love to press cookie cutters into cookie dough, and while I can guarantee you'll have dough and flour everywhere, you'll also have great memories forever. Five- and six-year-olds can certainly help to measure ingredients and dump them in bowls, and even drop spoonfuls of dough on cookie sheets. By age nine or ten, they should be able to make simple cookie recipes by themselves, even if you need to hover near the mixer and teach them safety rules, such as never inserting a spoon or scraper into the mixer while it is on. And taking trays in and out of the oven can be mastered somewhere along the way when you judge they can do so without burning themselves or harming the house.

The 4-H club program popular in many rural areas used to have children begin learning to cook with cookies and then tackle more difficult projects in subsequent years: muffins and quick bread in year two, and so on. And 4-H has kept up with the times. In my research about what is currently used in 4-H cooking programs, I found the youngest club members making healthy items like cheese kabobs and fruity shakes, and advancing to veggie pizzas and breakfast burritos in the older years. They provide fun and healthy recipes for things like oven-baked sweet potato fries in light olive oil and seasoning, and "Ants-on-a-Log" snacks of celery, cream cheese or peanut butter, and raisins.

Once kids get started in cooking, they often take off on their own. My sister-in-law's family was snowbound this year on her birthday in early February. I called her the next day to wish her a happy birthday. Then I consoled her for not being able to go out to eat. "Oh, Anna [her daughter, fifteen] made her first chocolate cake completely from scratch," Barbara said. "It was so good, today she wanted to make another one."

No one wants to curb such enthusiasm. Build on the natural interest your kids have in cooking and you won't be eating manna every day; you may have to eat homemade chocolate cake every day!

• • • • • • • • • •

Snowball Cookies

Melodie Davis

These are the cookies mentioned in the cookie disaster story in this chapter. Some people call these "wedding cakes" when pressed flat, but we like the little round, ridiculously rich snowballs. Children love to help form the snowballs and dust them with powdered sugar.

1½ cup / 375 ml butter, softened
¾ teaspoon salt
1½ cup / 375 ml chopped pecans or walnuts
½ cup / 125 ml sugar
2¼ teaspoons vanilla
3 cups / 750 ml flour
3 teaspoons water
Powdered sugar for dusting

Preheat oven to 325° F / 160° C. Cream butter and sugar. Add vanilla, flour, salt, water, and nuts. Form into balls the size of walnuts. Bake for 30–40 minutes on ungreased cookie sheets. Do not brown. Remove from pan. Cool 10 minutes. Roll each cookie in powdered sugar.

Whole Grain Chocolate Chip Cookies

Jodi Nisly Hertzler

I found this recipe years ago on the back of a bag of Safeway-brand chocolate chips, of all places. I love that these delicious cookies use only whole wheat flour and also have oatmeal and walnuts for a little added nutrition. As a bonus, they keep well in the freezer and stay soft for ages—the perfect cookie for lunchbox and after-school treats.

1 cup / 250 ml butter, softened
1 cup / 250 ml brown sugar
2 large eggs
1½ cup / 375 ml whole wheat flour
1 teaspoon baking soda
1 teaspoon salt
2 cups / 500 ml chocolate chips
2 cups / 500 ml quick-cooking oatmeal
1 teaspoon vanilla
1 cup / 250 ml chopped walnuts or pecans

Preheat oven to 375° F / 190° C.

Cream together the butter and sugar. Add eggs and beat well. In a separate bowl, stir together flour, soda, and salt. Add to butter mixture and beat. Stir in chocolate chips, oatmeal, vanilla, and nuts. Blend thoroughly. Drop by the tablespoon onto a greased cookie sheet. Bake 8–10 minutes.

No-Bake Bars

Lois Priest

Mom and I make these every year when we do our Christmas baking. They are a family favorite.

4 cups / 1 L Cheerios
2 cups / 500 ml crisp rice cereal
2 cups / 500 ml dry roasted peanuts
2 cups / 500 ml M&Ms or chocolate chips
1 cup / 250 ml light corn syrup
1 cup / 250 ml sugar
1½ cup / 375 ml creamy peanut butter
1 teaspoon salt
1 teaspoon vanilla

Grease a 15x10x1-inch baking pan. In a large bowl, combine the first four ingredients; set aside. In a saucepan, bring corn syrup and sugar to a boil. Cook and stir just until sugar is dissolved. Remove from heat. Stir in peanut butter, salt, and vanilla. Pour over the cereal mixture, and toss to coat evenly. Spread into the pan. Cool, then cut into squares.

Variation: Since M&Ms tend to melt somewhat, press them into the top of the mixture after spreading it into the pan, *but* do this before the mixture cools, or they won't stick.

Blondies

Carmen Wyse

This is a recipe I made all the time as a kid. After I was married and had my own children, I found it again. Now it is my go-to recipe for any time I need to take snacks to a kids event. I also make it a lot for potlucks. I rarely bring any back.

2 cups / 500 ml flour
¼ teaspoon baking powder
¼ teaspoon baking soda
1 teaspoon salt
⅓ cup / 75 ml butter, melted
2 cups / 500 ml brown sugar
2 eggs
2 teaspoons vanilla

Preheat oven to 350° F / 180° C. Mix together dry ingredients. Make a well and pour in melted butter, beaten eggs, and vanilla. Mix together. Batter will be very thick and pull away from the bowl to form a ball.

Put in an ungreased 9x13-inch pan. Use your hands to press it out into the pan. Sprinkle chocolate chips on top, if desired. Bake for 20–25 minutes.

Magic Cookie Bars

Melodie Davis

My husband's favorite Christmas treat. Easy to make, and you dirty only one cake pan. The recipe is from a condensed milk can and a high-school home economics class.

½ cup / 125 ml butter or margarine
1½ cup / 375 ml graham cracker crumbs
1 cup / 250 ml chopped nuts
1 cup / 250 ml chocolate or butterscotch chips (or ½ cup / 125 ml
    of each)
1⅓ cup / 325 ml shredded coconut
1 15-ounce / 450 g can sweetened condensed milk

Preheat oven to 350° F / 180° C. Melt butter or margarine in a 9x13 pan in the oven as it preheats. Crumb graham crackers with rolling pin until you have 1½ cup. (Put crackers in an old bread bag and take a rolling pin to them.) Sprinkle graham cracker crumbs over the melted butter or margarine as evenly as you can. Sprinkle on the chopped nuts, then chocolate or butterscotch bits, then coconut, then drizzle the condensed milk over the whole mixture.

Bake for 25 minutes. Cool 15 minutes, then cut into bars. Be sure to cut and remove within 15 minutes, or they stick badly to the pan.

Gingerbread Cookies

Jodi Nisly Hertzler

Every year in November, my kids ask if we can make gingerbread people, a request I used to dread. So often, the dough requires refrigeration, and before we're done rolling it out and cutting it into shapes, it's sticking to everything and nearly impossible to work with, and we all end up frustrated. I finally found this recipe online (I've changed it a bit), and I'll never use another one. The dough is amazingly pliable and easy to work with.

⅔ cup / 150 ml molasses
⅔ cup / 150 ml brown sugar
2 tablespoons ground ginger
3 teaspoons ground cinnamon
1 teaspoon ground allspice
1 teaspoon ground cloves
2 teaspoons baking soda
2 sticks (1 cup) unsalted butter, cut into tablespoon pieces
1 large egg, lightly beaten
3¾–4 cups / 925 ml–1 L flour
½ teaspoon salt

Bring molasses, brown sugar, and spices to a boil in a heavy saucepan over medium heat, stirring occasionally, until sugar is absorbed and mixture is hot. Remove from heat. Stir in baking soda (mixture will foam up), then stir in butter 3 pieces at a time, letting each addition melt before adding the next, until all butter is melted. Add egg and stir until combined, then stir in 3¾ cups flour and the salt.

Preheat oven to 325° F / 160° C. Transfer dough to a lightly floured surface and knead, dusting with as much of the remaining ¼ cup of flour as needed to prevent sticking, until soft and easy to handle (30 seconds to 1 minute). Wrap half of the dough in plastic wrap and keep at room temperature.

Roll out remaining dough to 1/8-inch thick on a lightly floured surface. Cut out as many cookies as possible and carefully transfer to 2 greased baking sheets, arranging them about 1 inch apart. Bake cookies in upper and lower thirds of oven, switching position of sheets halfway through baking, until edges are slightly darker, 10–12 minutes (watch carefully toward the end, because they burn easily). Transfer cookies to racks to cool completely. Make more cookies with remaining dough and scraps. Decorate as you like.

10

• • • • • • • • •

Getting Kids to Like Okra and Moo Goo Gai Pan

The writer of a travel column ventured down some back roads in the southern United States and discovered Virginia's delicious Brunswick stew (recipe in chapter 8). He described it as "succotash with mystery meat." Usually the meat today is chicken; in olden times, it might have been squirrel or rabbit. Further south, he sampled fried okra for the first time.

I remember when both of those dishes were new to me too. When I was growing up, my family considered pizza to be exotic food. I remember my first "pizza pie," served at a friend's home. I didn't like it. Then my elementary school in Middlebury, Indiana, started serving it, and I survived pizza day at first by just eating the crust off the bottom—no sauce. Then I began eating the cheese off the top. Eventually I learned to pick the ground beef out of the sauce. Finally I gave up and just ate the whole thing, and the rest is history: today pizza is a meal I love in most of its varied forms.

One woman told me that at about the same time in the fifties, her mother used to eat tacos off neighborhood taco trucks in California. While tacos have long lost their exotic sound, such trucks did not make an appearance in rural Virginia until the first decade of the 2000s.

Most of us no longer have to go to distant lands or even large cities to sample cuisine from around the world. Our relatively small town of forty thousand now has three Indian restaurants, two Thai, one Vietnamese, several Italian, and one each of Ethiopian, Cuban, Peruvian, Caribbean, Japanese, and others. I'm guessing conservatively that we have at least two dozen Chinese restaurants or take-outs. "Mexican" restaurants also abound. Taco stands are commonplace.

In my hometown of Goshen, Indiana, there was one lone Chinese restaurant when I was a kid, and it seemed as alien to me as a visit to the Great Wall would have been. On my first visit to that restaurant, I ordered an American hamburger, much to the chagrin of my aunt, who wanted me to sample the wonderful Chinese food. At school I would survive chop suey day by eating only the chow mein noodles sprinkled on the top of the pretty dreadful canned cafeteria stuff. I know it was dreadful, because we were required to at least try it.

So you get the idea that my palate was not extremely wide when I was a kid, but now I'll try most anything once. My Spanish professor in Barcelona shamed me into trying calamari (fried squid), and I ended up liking it. At a French restaurant in Winnipeg, I ate snails for the first time when my boss ordered them for our table of four as an appetizer. In a rich buttery sauce, they were amazingly delicious and not icky.

What can you do if your child balks at new foods? We cannot promote pleasant family mealtimes without also tackling this number-one difficult mealtime issue for many families.

In the 2009 book *My Two-Year-Old Eats Octopus*, author Nancy Tringali Piho contends that there is a lot of dumbing down when it comes to expectations about what kids will eat. She points to the short menu options for children in restaurants and fast-food places as shaping their and our outlook. These menus usually consist of grilled cheese, chicken nuggets, burgers, and pasta.[1] Early and overuse of salt, fat, and sugar can also hide or neutralize the real flavors of better foods. One of the many examples that Piho gives is canned or bottled pasta sauces: many are good, but are also very high in sodium.

The same is true of just about every canned soup on the market. Making homemade versions of any of these can lower the amount of sodium in the dish.

According to Piho, a mother's diet can influence the variety of flavors a child has been exposed to in the uterus and during breastfeeding. Researchers have even found that the less sweet the formula you give a baby is, the more inclined he or she will be to like less sweet foods later.[2]

I cannot overstate the importance of parents' expectations. If children hear that they are picky eaters, why would they want to disappoint their parents' or grandparents' expectations? If children know that they can get lots of attention by not eating certain foods, and if they like that attention, what incentive is there to learn to eat a food without complaining?

My kids went through a phase when they were quite picky. My standard response was, "Well, I guess your taste buds for that just haven't come in yet. But they will. Eventually you will like this food." I don't know how scientific or truthful that is, but it makes sense to me as a way to describe to children that they will learn later in life to like foods they don't like now. When we lay out that expectation for them, it can help.

I should confess that as an adult I do not like all foods either. I guess my taste buds still haven't developed for liver, caviar, anchovies, pâtés, and things along those lines. I already get enough calories and have enough trouble with weight that I don't feel motivated to try to learn to like them, thank you very much.

Mostly we need patience to get through the picky years and not make food a constant battleground. I have admired parents who calmly admit that a visiting child probably won't eat anything but the bread I serve at a meal, and I do not make an issue of it. The child will probably survive that meal and many more, if he or she is given enough options and some good multivitamins.

On the first Sunday of summer, our pastor asked the children if there were any foods they look forward to eating during the summertime. She was fully expecting to hear either ice cream or watermelon (for ice cream was the point of her illustration), but one four-year-old boy responded at the top of his lungs, "Broccoli!" Most of us were so stunned we broke out in laughter. I wonder if poor Ethan wondered what was so funny. This is another indication that our food expectations for children are too limiting. Even my chapter title makes that assumption.

But we need to remember that *all* children start out as picky eaters: they eat one food—mother's milk or formula. Every food they encounter beyond that is a *new* food, something that may have to be an acquired taste. I heard someone suggest it takes about five to six taste trials to get to like a new food.

My children heard the "your taste buds just haven't come in yet" line from me so often that I'm sure they hated me for it, yet it seems to be true. How else would you explain to a child that foods most of us didn't like as children are now favorites.

I spent a year in Mennonite Voluntary Service right out of high school. Sitting at the table of the hostess, who did most of our cooking (this was 1970, we weren't very liberated about roles then), I tasted for the first time a multitude of foods I came to love: tuna, shrimp, broccoli, Brussels sprouts, cottage cheese, and lasagna. These were things my mother never made. My husband, whose aunts say he survived childhood on peanut butter and jelly sandwiches, learned to like many of the foods I served through the years.

Many of us owe a huge debt to Doris Janzen Longacre and her *More-with-Less Cookbook* for expanding our palates. That book made its appearance just when I was graduating from college, and it was one of my treasured gifts as a bride in 1976. My ventures into cooking foods from around the world mostly come from those pages.

More-with-Less Cookbook has an easy and good homemade tortilla recipe that, once tried, makes it hard to be satisfied eating store-bought tortillas. As is often the case, being out of something and not wanting to run to the store to get it was the reason I first tried that recipe. My daughter Tanya had invited friends over at the spur of the moment, and we decided to make tacos, only to discover I had only a few frozen tortillas on hand. So I dug out *More-with-Less*, turned to page 84 (it's still on page 84 in the

2000 edition), and was surprised at how easy they were to make. Tanya's friends loved them.

If you can make pie crust or biscuits, you can make homemade tortillas. (Carmen provides a tortilla recipe in chapter 1.) Give the children their own little dough balls, and let them roll them as thin as they can. Most kids will like the taste of a warm, fresh tortilla, bland and neutral. Gradually you can introduce them to melting cheese in it for a simple quesadilla. From there their tastes and desires will branch out, and they will explore adding refried beans, ground beef with flavorings, tomatoes, mild salsa, and so on.

My last-minute-guests crisis and first try at making tortillas brings to mind the quick meal Sarah is asked to prepare one day when three visitors suddenly appear at Abraham and Sarah's tent (see Genesis 18:1-15). These are heavenly visitors, because the passage starts with "The LORD appeared to Abraham . . . while he was sitting at the entrance to his tent in the heat of the day. Abraham looked up and saw three men standing nearby." Abraham hurries to get Sarah and asks her to bake some bread. He has a servant kill a calf, and as they consume the meal, Abraham finds out the main reason for the visit: the prediction of he and Sarah having a son. Sarah's hurried meals fades to the background as she hears the joyful and preposterous news: even at her age, she will have a son. (Incidentally, that son, Isaac, grows up to be a player in one of the Bible's most significant food stories, which we looked at in chapter 5.)

Being willing to make foods from scratch, substituting different ingredients if you don't have something a recipe calls for, and opening yourself to whatever visitors happen to come your way are all ways to help your children grow up with a willingness to experiment with and enjoy food, and to demonstrate hospitality to their friends and others. Opening ourselves to new foods as adults can be a way of opening ourselves to new peoples and cultures, and the foods they love.

● ● ● ● ● ● ● ● ● ●

Chicken and Beans in Red Curry

Carmen Wyse

I was introduced to a wonderful dish at our local Thai restaurant and thought a lot about trying to recreate it. I found two recipes online that seemed a good starting place, combined them and added a bit of my own, and came up with this. It turned out very close to the restaurant dish. Red curry paste is very spicy, so judge how much to use based on your family's preferences.

2 skinless chicken breasts, thinly sliced
1 pound / 500 g green beans
1 tablespoon olive or peanut oil
1–3 tablespoon red curry paste (personal taste)
1 onion, small, chopped
3 garlic cloves, mined
1 teaspoon fresh ginger, grated
1 13½-ounce can / 400 g coconut milk (or light)
3 tablespoons fish sauce
2 tablespoons sugar
½–1 cup / 125–250 ml fresh basil leaves, loosely packed
        (Thai basil, if you have it) (optional)
½ lime, squeezed

Heat oil in large pan. Add curry paste and stir until bubbling. Add onions, garlic, and ginger. Sauté 1–2 minutes. Add chicken slices and brown on one side. Flip chicken and add green beans on top. Cook for 2–3 minutes. (Optional: Cover to help cook green beans.)

Completely mix in green beans. Add coconut milk, fish sauce, and sugar. Simmer for 5–10 minutes. Test green beans to your personal crunch preference. Mix in basil leaves and fresh lime juice right before serving. Serve over brown rice.

Enchiladas

Emily Ralph

Like many newlyweds, my parents were dirt poor in the first years of their marriage. They loved Mexican food, but couldn't afford to go to their favorite restaurant. My mom spent hours in the kitchen experimenting until she created the perfect enchilada—and this has become a favorite family recipe.

1 pound / 500 g ground beef (or shredded roast beef, chicken, or turkey)
3 tablespoons minced onion
1 16-ounce / 500 g can pinto beans
2 teaspoons cumin
1 teaspoon chili powder
1 teaspoon garlic salt
10 8-inch / 20 cm flour tortillas
1 pound / 500 g grated cheese (cheddar, marble, or Monterey Jack)

Ranchero sauce:
2 cups beef or chicken broth
2 tablespoons minced onion
2 tablespoons cornstarch
1 teaspoon cumin
½ teaspoon chili powder
½ teaspoon garlic salt

Brown ground beef with onion. Puree beans in food processor or crush with potato masher. Mix beans, meat, cumin, chili powder, and garlic salt. Divide mixture equally among the 10 tortillas, then roll tortillas up. Place in 9x13 baking dish.

Mix ingredients for ranchero sauce in microwavable bowl. Heat in microwave until mixture boils. Whisk until smooth. Pour over tortillas. Cover enchiladas with grated cheese. Bake at 350° F / 180° C for 25–30 minutes or until cheese is melted and sauce is bubbling. Top with sour cream. Serve with refried beans and rice.

Falafel

Jodi Nisly Hertzler

These little fried chickpea cakes are easy and delicious, but they do take a little planning ahead. The chickpeas need at least eight hours of soaking time, and then you need to make the mix and refrigerate it a couple of hours. But if you plan it right (start soaking the chickpeas at night, make the mix in the morning, and fry them for supper), they make a delightful meal. Kids may like dipping them in ranch dressing.

1 cup / 250 ml dried chickpeas
½ large onion, roughly chopped (about 1 cup /250 ml)
2 tablespoons finely chopped fresh parsley
2 tablespoons finely chopped fresh cilantro
1 teaspoon salt
½–1 teaspoon red pepper flakes
4 cloves of garlic, smashed
1 teaspoon cumin
1 teaspoon baking powder
4–6 tablespoons flour
Soybean or vegetable oil for frying
Pita bread
Toppings, including chopped tomato, shredded lettuce, chopped
          cucumbers, diced onion, diced green pepper
Tahini sauce (below)

Put the chickpeas in a large bowl, and add enough cold water to cover them by at least 2 inches. Let soak overnight, then drain. (Don't use canned chickpeas; they won't hold together.)

Place the drained, uncooked chickpeas and onions in the bowl of a food processor. Add parsley, cilantro, salt, red pepper flakes, garlic, and cumin. Process until blended but not pureed. Sprinkle in the baking powder and 4 tablespoons of the flour, and pulse. Add enough flour so that the dough forms a small ball and no longer sticks to your hands. Turn into a bowl and refrigerate, covered, for several hours.

Form the chickpea mixture into balls about the size of a ping-pong ball. Heat 3 inches of oil to 375° F / 190° C in a deep pot or wok, and fry 1 ball to test. If it falls apart, add a little flour. Fry about 6 balls at once for a few minutes on each side, or until golden brown. Drain on paper towels. Stuff half a pita with falafel balls and the veggies. Drizzle with tahini sauce (below).

Tahini Sauce

½ cup / 125 ml tahini (sesame seed paste—next to peanut butter
    in larger grocery stores)
½ cup / 125 ml plain yogurt
1–2 lemons, juiced (to taste)
2 garlic cloves, diced
1 teaspoon fresh parsley, chopped
½ teaspoon salt
Pinch paprika

Combine all the ingredients in a blender, process on high speed to make a smooth and creamy sauce. Adjust seasoning to taste, and serve with falafels or as a salad dressing. Makes about 1 cup / 250 ml.

North African Couscous with Shrimp

Carmen Wyse

3 tablespoons olive oil
1 large red bell pepper, chopped
8–10 scallions, sliced
5 cloves garlic, minced or pressed
2 teaspoons ground coriander
1 teaspoon turmeric
¼ teaspoon of cayenne, or to taste
1 quart / 1 L hot chicken stock
1 pound / 500 g shelled shrimp
2 cups / 500 ml fresh or frozen peas
2 cups / 500 ml couscous
2 tablespoons butter or margarine
Salt and pepper to taste
Sliced almonds, toasted*
Chopped fresh parsley
Lemon wedges

Heat oil in a large saucepan. Add the peppers, scallions, garlic, coriander, turmeric, and cayenne. Sauté over medium heat for 3–4 minutes, stirring occasionally. Stir in the chicken stock. Add the shrimp, and cook for another 3–4 minutes, until the shrimp is pink. Stir in the peas and cook for another minute. Mix in the couscous and butter or margarine. Cover, remove from heat, and let stand for 5 minutes. Uncover the pan and, using a fork, fluff up the couscous and break up any lumps. Add salt and pepper to taste. Serve on a platter, topped with toasted almonds, parsley, and lemon wedges.

*Toasting almonds: Pile them on a small plate and microwave 30 seconds. Stir and do it again. Continue until they are toasted well.

Zanzibar Coconut Fish Soup

Carmen Wyse

My parents spent ten years in Africa and acquired several African cookbooks while there. This recipe came from a collection from various restaurants in Africa. In the original recipe, you make coconut milk by pouring hot water over a coconut. It also has you making fish stock from scratch. This adaptation is much simpler but still tasty.

1 can (13.5-oz) / 400 g coconut milk
3–4 tablespoons canola or peanut oil
1 pound white fish, cut into ½-inch cubes
½ cup / 125 ml celery, finely chopped
½ cup / 125 ml leeks, finely chopped
1 medium onion, finely chopped
1 teaspoon curry powder
Salt and pepper to taste
1 teaspoon chopped garlic
½ green chili pepper, chopped
3 cups / 750 ml fish (preferred) or chicken stock
1 can chopped tomatoes
¼ cup / 50 ml cilantro, chopped
Juice of 1–2 limes

Heat oil in a large saucepan. Add fish cubes, celery, leeks, and onions, and fry for 3–4 minutes. Add curry powder, salt, pepper, garlic, and chili, and sauté for another minute or so. Stir in coconut milk and fish or chicken stock. Add tomatoes and simmer for 10 minutes. Throw in the chopped cilantro and lime juice just before serving.

Alfajores

Carmen Wyse

2 cups / 500 ml flour
1 cup / 250 ml (2 sticks) butter, softened
½ cup / 125 ml sugar
2 egg yolks
½ teaspoon salt
1 can sweetened condensed milk

Dulce de leche:

Remove label from condensed milk can. Put can of milk in a pan of water—with water covering the top of the can—and simmer 4–5 hours. Keep a kettle of hot water on the stove and add hot water as needed to keep the can covered. Cool before opening. (Consider doing this the day before.)

Cookies:

Preheat oven to 350° F / 180° C. Cream the butter and sugar. Add egg yolks, then stir in flour and salt. You will have a very soft dough. Roll out on a floured board to about ⅛-inch thick. Cut into circles—not too big, because these are rich. Bake for 8–10 minutes, just until they start turning golden around the edges (just a hint of color starting).

Once cool, spread dulce de leche on a cookie, and make a sandwich with another cookie. Cover with powdered sugar. Makes about 2½ dozen 1½-inch diameter sandwich cookies.

Tip: Save leftover dulce de leche to spread on apple slices for a simple and delicious dessert or after-school treat.

11

. . . .

Eating All Day for the Price of One Grande Caffè Latte

In 2001 a book came out that caught my eye: *Not Just Beans: 50 Years of Frugal Family Favorites* by Tawra Kellam (now titled *Dining on a Dime*). This author made an ambitious claim: save seven thousand dollars in one year without working extra. I was intrigued.

Among the food items the author cut out of her budget, for example, were the following (recalculated to my own context in 2010):

- One $3 bag of potato chips each week saved $156 per year.
- A weekly $4 box of cereal, $208 a year.
- A weekly restaurant meal for two people at $40 a meal, $2,080 annually.
- One less delivered pizza per week at $20, save $1,040.
- No daily gourmet coffee at $3 a cup, $1,095.
- No daily liter of soda, $365.
- No daily pack of snack cakes, $455.
- One less bottle of water per day, $455.
- 1 cup less juice per person in a family of four, $546.

- 3 pounds less red meat a week, $468.
- Bag lunch instead of eating out, $5 a day (5 days a week for 50 weeks a year), $1,250.[1]

At 2010 prices, these all add up to over eight thousand dollars a year. At first I thought, *Wow*. Then I realized that we rarely eat anywhere that costs forty dollars a meal: if we eat out, it's fast food for fifteen bucks. If we cut back one less delivered pizza a week, we wouldn't be eating any pizza—which might be a good idea. Or if we cut back one box of cereal, what are we supposed to eat? My excuses went on. But I think the list is worth looking at, because most of us can find several things to try.

My parents were frugal farmers, but they did enjoy travel and were generous in contributing to world missions and relief efforts. For one special trip, they traveled around the world, visiting mission sites and relief distribution centers, and attending the Mennonite World Conference. Dad always said he paid for that trip by not smoking cigarettes or drinking alcohol. Technically, a couple of his prime hogs paid for the trip with their lives, but that's another story.

Speaking of cheap, the best way to save money when eating out is to always order just water to drink. We can be thankful that tap water is still offered free almost everywhere in North America, which isn't the case in all countries. For a family of four eating out once a week, ordering just water easily saves five hundred dollars a year; it amounts to 10- to 20-percent off the price of your meal, and thus pays the tip. Who wouldn't go for a deal like that? Sometimes I want coffee with my dessert, and so I splurge, but my drink of choice in most restaurants is good old calorie-free water.

During tough times, most families can save a bundle by cooking and eating at home. In fact, at the time of this writing—a period of recession—home cooking seems to be coming back. The popularity of various cooking shows on the Food Channel is one indicator of people interested in cooking at home. *Everyday Food* on PBS and its related magazine purports to feature meals and foods that average families would actually cook—as opposed to thirty-five-ingredient recipes you'd never have time for.

Soups are one of my favorite ways to enjoy a tasty and nutritious meal while being kind to our budget. A creative cook can make soup out of almost anything, or almost nothing. One day, my daughter was hungry for chicken noodle soup. While I make many homemade soups, Campbell's Homestyle Chicken Noodle Soup in the "Heart Healthy" version is lower in sodium and for us a delicious staple for hurried and harried days. But somehow I'd run out. I did have a number of containers of saved chicken broth in the freezer from various chicken meals, but I couldn't find any leftover chicken or proper egg noodles.

We quickly threw together a tasty homemade soup out of thin spaghetti noodles broken into three-inch lengths; frozen broth; bits of celery, onion, and carrots; salt; pepper; and celery seed. I left a celery stalk with leaves simmer with the broth for about twenty minutes. The resulting soup was lovely. Our only mistake: we should have left the spaghetti noodles long for easier eating or broken them into smaller pieces so they'd fit in the spoon instead of sliding off.

Vegetable soups can be a wonderful way of cleaning out the freezer of all those dribbles of leftover green beans, corn, peas, and limas. While I grew up on canned vegetable soup, I never buy it myself; generally homemade soups are so much better and thriftier. The "chunky" soups that are popular now are delicious, but I gulp to pay a dollar and a half or more for a can.

Especially during winter, nothing warms and satisfies like a good, hearty soup: vegetable, chili, broccoli, bean, potato, chicken noodle, or corn chowder. It is truly comfort food. Anything except something fishy or clammy—but maybe my taste buds for those will come in someday.

I do not claim to be especially frugal, nor is my family particularly noteworthy for getting by on less. We try to save where we can, but we also wouldn't win any thrift awards. I would say my efforts at frugality are affected more by the lifestyles of my friends, family, colleagues, and church friends than by great discipline or resolve on my part.

Some moms and dads seem to be able to accomplish miraculous feedings on just pennies. After the earthquake in Haiti in early 2010, bestselling author Mitch Albom had a piece in

Parade magazine, talking about commonalities he found with teens in Haiti on an earlier mission trip. One Haitian friend said he once had ten American dollars, which he lived on for a *month*. Haitian families ate rice and beans every night. Most of our families would complain about that diet.[2]

This brings to mind the biblical story of Elijah staying with a widow at Zarephath (see 1 Kings 17:7-24): There has been no rain in the land for quite a while; indeed, Elijah has been fed by ravens because there is so little food. God tells Elijah to go to Zarephath, and a widow will supply him with food.

In Zarephath, Elijah sees a woman gathering sticks to make a fire, and he first asks for a little water and some bread. "As surely as the LORD your God lives, I don't have any bread," the woman says, "only a handful of flour in a jar and a little oil in a jug. I am gathering a few sticks to take home and make a meal for myself and my son, that we may eat it—and die."

Elijah responds, "Go home and do as you have said, but first make a small cake of bread for me . . . and bring it to me, and then make something for yourself and your son." And then Elijah promises that God will not allow the jar of flour to be used up or the jug of oil to run dry until some more rain falls on the land.

The woman's faith and faithfulness not only gets her and her family through the drought and crisis, but later, when her son appears to die, Elijah miraculously restores him to life (or God does).

I always loved this story as a child. That jug of oil and jar of flour never running out was magical to me. Today it speaks to me of the importance of keeping a good supply of basics in your pantry and having the know-how to use them: flour and oil and water are all that are needed to make a tortilla—a nice reminder of Elijah's life-sustaining cakes.

Many people in North America feed their pets better and more expensive food than what many of our global neighbors live on. Jeff Carr, a young seminary intern at the time, and now pastor of a large congregation, got our congregation buzzing the day he brought an opened can of dog food to church for his children's sermon. He proceeded to tell the children that since he was commuting back and forth from his seminary to our church on weekends, he hadn't had time for breakfast that morning. He was hoping they wouldn't mind if he ate his breakfast during the children's sermon.

Jeff asked the children if any of them had ever eaten dog food. One girl volunteered that her father had—and from his seat the father laughingly confirmed it, but that it was a doggy biscuit.

Jeff got out a plastic fork, stuffed a napkin in his shirt, read the label on the can, and said, "It says it has all these vitamins and minerals, so it must be good and nutritious." Then he proceeded to stab a piece of the food and pop it into his mouth.

I confess my stomach was a little queasy at this point, but Jeff proceeded to pop another morsel into his mouth and pronounce it "delicious." He didn't seem to flinch or grimace as he swallowed.

Then he came clean. "This is really a candy bar," he confessed, to the disappointment and envy of the children and the relief of the adults in the room. He reminded them that they should never "judge a book by its cover" and always remember to try to look on the inside of a person before judging them by their appearance. An apt lesson for us all.

When Jeff started in with his dog-food illustration, I thought he was going to remind us that there are people in poverty who have to eat dog food. At least I have heard stories of elderly people eating dog food. While I don't know personally anyone putting cans of dog food on the table during times of recession, I know that hunger, even in the United States and Canada, is a real problem. Many depend on food pantries to stretch thin food budgets, even while holding down a low-paying job. Our efforts to be frugal and thrifty should result in more wealth not just to stockpile but to share.

So can you really eat all day for the price of one Grande Caffè Latte? We currently have three people in our household and together we spend an average of 125 dollars a week on groceries and maybe two modest meals out. That boils down to $1.95 a day per person. (It does not factor in what we spend on gardening.) We enjoy fresh fruits and vegetables in season, and we sometimes splurge, guiltily, on such goodies out of season. And since my husband wants meat seven days a week, our budget allows for that too.

While I watch my pennies, I purchase whatever I feel like buying at the grocery store or farmers market. We grow and preserve our own tomatoes, green beans, peas, corn, potatoes, and pickles to use all year, but we have not advanced to what I consider the more elaborate food preservation practices of drying and canning fruits or preserves, or making grape or other juices. While I admire a family like Barbara Kingsolver's of *Animal, Vegetable, Miracle* fame, we aren't Kingsolvers, who grow much of their meat, make cheese, and spend hours every day through the summer and fall canning and preserving.

So yes, it is possible to eat on less than what some would spend daily on one cup of coffee. Many live on a lot less than *my* budget. Overall, food is still a great bargain for those living in North America. Those in the global south spend from 50 to 75 percent of their income on food, while persons in North America generally spend around 12 percent.[3]

We have much for which to be grateful, and responsible. If you incorporate just one new idea from this chapter for cutting back, making your own or sharing more, that is a worthy goal.

● ● ● ● ● ● ● ● ●

Pumpkin Soup

Burton Buller

I found a pumpkin soup recipe that I thought might be interesting to try. Only after I had mixed the ingredients did I notice that I had pulled a can of preseasoned, sweetened pumpkin pie filling from the pantry, not the plain, unseasoned pumpkin that the recipe called for. I decided to go ahead and finish the recipe in spite of my mistake. Upon tasting the result, I was pleased that I had made the mistake. This is a sweet soup—something very different, and oh so delectable.

1 medium onion
1 stalk celery
1 tablespoon butter
2½ cups / 625 ml chicken stock
1 cup / 250 ml pumpkin pie filling (preseasoned and sweetened,
     ready for the pie)
1 large carrot, grated
1 tablespoon honey
1/8 teaspoon each of ginger, cinnamon, allspice, clove, pepper
½ tablespoon cornstarch
1 cup / 250 ml milk
½ cup / 125 ml half-and-half
Salt to taste

Melt butter in a medium stockpot and add onion and celery. Sautee a few moments until tender, then add ½ cup chicken stock. Cook over medium heat for 5–6 minutes, stirring frequently. Add pumpkin, carrots, spices, and remaining broth. Stir to combine, and cook another 5–10 minutes. (At this point, puree, if desired.) Add milk and half-and-half. Bring to a slow boil. Add corn starch. Cook 2 more minutes or until thickened.

Cheese Chowder

Betty Hertzler

I found this recipe in a church cookbook, and it has become a family favorite. It's simple but tasty, and the perfect supper on a chilly evening.

Combine in a large pot and cook until vegetables are soft:
3 cups / 750 ml chicken stock or water
4 cups / 1 L potatoes, diced
1 cup / 250 ml celery, diced
1 cup / 250 ml carrots, diced
½ cup / 125 ml onion, diced
2 cloves garlic, diced
2 teaspoons salt
¼ teaspoon pepper

Add:
½ cup / 125 ml butter
1 quart / 1 L milk
½ cup / 125 ml flour dissolved in ½ cup water
1 pound / 500 g cheddar cheese, shredded
2 cups / 500 ml diced, cooked ham (optional)
Hot pepper sauce to taste

Crockpot Potato Soup

Kimberly Metzler

This isn't a thick soup like some potato soups, but we like it. How wonderful that it cooks all day while I'm away! My husband is always delighted when he finds this on the table at suppertime.

Combine in a slow cooker and cook on low for 7–8 hours, or until vegetables are tender:

6 cups / 1.5 L potatoes, peeled and cubed

5 cups / 1.3 L water

2 medium onions, chopped

½ cup / 125 ml celery, chopped

½ cup / 125 ml carrots, thinly sliced

¼ cup / 50 ml butter or margarine

4 teaspoons chicken bouillon granules

2 teaspoons salt

¼ teaspoon pepper

Before serving, stir in:

1 can (12 oz.) / 340 g evaporated milk

3 tablespoons fresh parsley, chopped (3 teaspoons dried)

Snipped chives (optional)

Top with shredded cheese and bacon bits.

Suggestion: If you prefer to avoid MSG, substitute chicken or vegetable broth for the water and chicken bouillon.

Tuscan Minestrone Soup

Jodi Nisly Hertzler

This recipe was given to me by a coworker when I was working at a middle school in Oregon. He had grown up in Brooklyn (and claimed to be a classmate of Tony Danza of Who's the Boss *and* Taxi *fame), and he told me that this is an old family recipe, considered a cure for many ailments.*

¼ cup / 50 ml olive oil
1 medium red onion, chopped
6 garlic cloves, peeled and whole
2 carrots, sliced
2–3 ribs celery, sliced
1 bunch kale, separated from stalk, rinsed and chopped, not too
          small (4–5 cups / 1–1.3 L chopped)
1 whole head or ½ large head green cabbage, chopped
1 can Italian-style diced tomatoes (11–14 oz / 335–420 g)
2 cans small white beans (11–14 oz / 335–420 g)
1 can pinto beans (11–14 oz / 335–420 g)
8 cups / 2 L chicken broth

Boil cabbage for 5 minutes to knock out the sour taste, which might taint the soup. Drain and rinse in cold water and set aside.

Sauté the garlic, onion, carrots, and celery in a large nonstick pot for 10 minutes, stirring occasionally. Add cooked cabbage and kale, and sauté until heated. Throw in the rest of the ingredients. Stir well and slowly. Bring to a simmer. Under low heat, cook for 2 hours for a soup with more broth or longer for a stew-like consistency. Serve with fresh grated Parmesan and crusty bread.

Lentil Casserole

Carmen Wyse

This recipe made it into our family cookbook twice. The original recipe uses a package of onion soup mix in place of the onion, garlic, carrots, salt, and soy sauce. Either way, it is easy, affordable, and delicious. I often take this to church potlucks and rarely have any left.

2 cups / 500 ml lentils
2 bay leaves
4 cups / 1 L water
½–1 pound / 250–500 g hamburger
2–3 tablespoons olive oil
1 onion, chopped
2 carrots, grated
3 cloves garlic, minced
1 teaspoon salt
⅛ teaspoon pepper
1 tablespoon soy sauce
¼ cup / 50 ml brown sugar
2 tablespoons molasses
2 tablespoons sweet pickle juice
1 cup / 250 ml water

Cook washed lentils in 4 cups water, uncovered, over medium heat for 30 minutes. In a bit of olive oil, sauté onion, garlic, and carrot. Add burger and brown. Add burger mixture to lentils along with the rest of the ingredients. Bake uncovered at 400° F / 200° C for 30 minutes or in the slow cooker 2–3 hours on high.

Dave Schrock's Tuna/Egg Skillet Dinner

Melodie Davis

This is a one- or two-person meal that I adapted from one of the guys who made it (greatly multiplied) for a houseful of students who lived in a big old house during my sophomore year at Eastern Mennonite University. That year of sharing one-dish meals with a long table of twelve to fourteen people was a glimpse of true community. This recipe serves one or two. So simple, but hearty and tasty, it is basically a variation of fried rice.

1 can tuna, drained
2 eggs
2 teaspoons margarine or olive oil
1 cup / 250 ml cooked rice (fix according to package directions)

Fry eggs in a skillet over medium heat, gently chopping them up with the side of a spatula so that the eggs are mixed and chopped (but not scrambled). Push eggs to the side of the skillet, so they won't get overly brown, while you brown tuna for 2–3 minutes, stirring. Add cooked rice. Stir tuna, eggs, and rice together, and brown several more minutes. Serve with soy sauce, if desired.

12

• • • • • • • • •

How Food, Packaging, and Waste Impact the Planet: What You Can Do

Aluminum pop cans. Beer bottles. Styrofoam coffee cups. Kentucky Fried Chicken boxes, with bones. Cellophane. Plastic bags. Wrapping paper. Rope. Remains of soup in a Styrofoam bowl. The remnants of what had to have been a teenage beer party: about eighty beer bottles tossed over a fence into a field—still there after a year. And, since this is rural Virginia on a road frequented by hunters, at least six deer carcasses.

Feeling sick yet? Such was the inventory of roadside trash I saw one day. Did you notice how many of the items in the list have to do with food and its storage? Any look at dealing responsibly and creatively with family mealtimes today has to include a look at the issue of food packaging and storage of the food we end up throwing away.

I'm sure most readers of this book wouldn't dream of littering. Yet tens of thousands of people—maybe millions—obviously think nothing of it. When we were kids in rural Indiana more than fifty years ago, we littered too, maybe believing the wind would carry away the trash into the fields and away from sight. We hauled our tin cans and other trash to the woods to deteriorate and rot. But this was before there were quite so many cars on the road and people in the world. We simply were not aware. Today we know that things can and must change.

My daughter Michelle had what to me was an amusing discussion with two colleagues at her office in Washington, D.C. One was born and bred a city girl; the other grew up in a rural area of Jamaica. And Michelle grew up hauling our own trash to the landfill every couple of weeks—where it was covered by soil and plastic sealers and then vented so gases could escape.

The city colleague had had a dream about garbage on a barge being dumped into the ocean. She woke up wondering, *What do they do with trash, ultimately, anyway?* Actually, until about 1935, ocean dumping was indeed what happened to a lot of city trash. Today most of it goes to landfills, except for certain types of ocean disposal that are greatly regulated.

Michelle explained landfills to her friends, who to her surprise had no concept of what they were. She described how, when she was a child, the landfill was just a dump that was actually open to scavengers like our family, and we sometimes took home "finds." Her friends were intrigued. Michelle recalled one of her favorite toys hauled from the dump: a backyard merry-go-round with sliding seats that you pushed back and forth with the movement of your body.

The young Jamaican woman talked about burning almost all trash, but she wasn't talking so much about paper and refuse, as about discarded food and sugar cane. Michelle had a chance to do her own gaping in wonderment. Again, in an earlier time, many cities and even apartment buildings in the United States had their own huge incinerators, but pollution laws closed most down. Much city garbage in the northeastern United States now gets trucked out to landfills in Virginia, Pennsylvania, Ohio, and New Jersey.

Sadly, the amount of trash keeps increasing. The production of more goods ultimately destined for the landfill is what drives our— and the world's—economy. It gives us jobs, goods, and security. It allows travel and opportunities. Obviously we can't do away with all consumption and go back to "living off the land." But we can greatly reduce trash with recycling and reusing. When we were a family of five, we produced two hundred or more bagfuls of trash a year—about four a week. My household of three currently ends up with about one bag of trash a week.

What happens if production is removed from the economies of our communities? One summer, when our youngest daughter, Doreen, helped with an environmental study as part of an internship in southern Virginia, she told Stuart and me about the interconnectedness of a community, its economy, and the environment. In simplified terms, furniture factories of the area had begun to fail when production was outsourced overseas. Enormous factories were left vacant.

The local counties and cities in which they were located lost huge tax revenues. The local governments had to reduce their budgets and couldn't make much-needed repairs to sewer and water systems, which began to seep sewage into the land and streams. This was only *one* problem affecting stream health. Doreen counted certain bellwether bugs and organisms to determine how well or ill a stream actually was. The study confirmed that sewage contamination is not just a problem in developing countries of Africa and Asia.

Environmental and family mealtime issues are connected on many fronts. Let's begin with ten motivating factors as to why the ordinary person should care for the environment.

1. The water you drink will be safer.
2. The air you breathe will be cleaner.
3. The food you eat will be healthier.
4. The price of gas may be less.
5. The health of your community will be better.
6. You will save money (although sometimes it takes an initial outlay).
7. You may live longer.
8. You will make the world a more beautiful and pleasant place to live.
9. God says it's a good idea.
10. There is no planet B (to quote CastleHillWizard on Yahoo answers).

For the purposes of this chapter, let's focus on wise uses of food and water and then wend our way back to the issue of the family dinner table, which is so deeply connected to the environment.

As a child, I heard about the "population explosion" and thought we were in danger of not having enough square footage on earth to accommodate people. But as I traveled through places like the Smoky Mountains, the Rockies, the great open plains, the Ozarks, the wilds of upper Michigan and Canada, I thought, *How could all that space ever fill up?* The aquifers beneath North America seem vast and deep—let alone the oceans so huge you can't begin to see across them.

Now I understand that preserving the open space is critical to our planet's survival. We need land for growing food; forests to clean the air and provide homes for animals and birds, which have roles in our ecosystem; wetlands and healthy streams, lakes, rivers, and oceans for habitat for rich aquatic life. In short, if it's all concrete and macadam, humans can't survive.

Our insects and fish function as the canary in the coal mine that determines whether the air is safe for the miners. For forty-some years, Stuart fished the lakes, rivers, and streams of our beautiful Shenandoah Valley. Today he has almost given up fishing because recently the fish developed weird sores and began dying. People cried "agricultural run off." Cows, chickens, pigs, and horses have been here for at least a couple hundred years and, yes, there is more intense industrialized farming than there was fifty years ago, contributing to the river pollution. But it doesn't take an environmental scientist to look around at the massive commercial and residential development occurring in this once mainly agricultural valley to point out the negative role this development has played in polluting our waters.

So what's the answer? Zero population growth? That may be part of it (I can't say anything here because we raised three children), but certainly doing a better job of planning for modest, wise growth in keeping with the surrounding community is another part. Voting for politicians who care about not destroying wetlands, farmlands, and forests is another part. (Good luck with that: we all know how developers' money talks in zoning meetings and in the back rooms.)

Mostly, caring about this issue and doing all the little daily things contribute to a cleaner, greener earth.[1] It means working, as those in southern Virginia have, to bring new information-age and service jobs to the local economy to sustain a tax base to fix and update old sewer systems. We can't wait for an environmental doomsday; we have to take action every day—now.

How?

In pioneer days, there was virtually no packaging for items bought in the town's general store. Goods were wrapped with plain paper or deposited in the tins, bags, or jars brought by the customer. Paper, string, and any packaging was diligently saved and reused till it fell apart. There were many fewer goods: today we have fifty different cold remedies, fifty types of potato chips, fifty types of bread. In unfamiliar grocery stores, I look down a long aisle and feel discouraged before I begin: where will I ever find the product I'm looking for?

Somewhere there's a happy medium between the vacant shelves of stores in old communist-run countries and shelves of North American stores, with their fifty types of toilet bowl cleaner. I make that comparison because I'll never forget the Russian visitor to our home just after the opening of the borders of the former Soviet Union in the 1980s. She couldn't get over the vast selection in our stores and at a restaurant's buffet table.

Somewhere there's a happy medium between no birthday or Christmas gifts or just an orange—and a half-dozen or more new items given to *each* child for *each* gift-giving occasion. Such consumption adds up, especially when you have a couple of children.

You don't have to "just say no." Just do less. Do less buying, less wasting, less disposing. It may be a drop in the bucket, but everyone's drops add up. Each effort means more space in the landfill and more time until we have to start a new one. In the last ten years, reusable shopping bags have become commonplace, and shopping at farmers markets has encouraged minimal packaging. Reusing our plastic food containers for leftovers and freezing dribbles of things helps save on plastic wrap and foil. Recycling everything possible—plastic, paper, cardboard, aluminum, tin, and glass—keeps trash to a minimum.

For Christians, wise use of the earth's resources is not something we do as a social cause. It is not a political or scientific endeavor or statement. It is a Christian calling. The purpose of all our activities on earth—and life in general—is to bring glory to God. In the opening pages of the Bible, we find the description of creation and the command to take care of it. How we eat and live makes a difference in how much land and food is available to fulfill Jesus' call to feed the hungry of the world. In the *More-with-Less Cookbook*, Doris Janzen Longacre put it this way: "The whole grains, legumes, vegetables and fruits, and moderate amounts of animal products that make sense in light of world food needs are also the best for our health. When we reduce our need for heavily grain-fed meat, the super-processed, the sugary, we not only release resources for the hungry, but also protect our own health and pocketbooks."[2]

• • • • • • • • •

Probably one of the best known of miracle stories in the Bible is the feeding of the five thousand—the only miracle story told in all four Gospels, apart from the resurrection. Usually our focus in this story—and the feeding of the four thousand in Matthew 15—is on the way God turns a small meal into one that feeds thousands of people.

But why does Matthew take time to record the *leftovers* (Matthew 14:20; 15:37)? Did the disciples pick up the leftovers only to discard them somewhere? Did they pick up the bread because they didn't want to litter? Was it simply to show the bounty of the miraculous feeding? I'm sure there were many poor or hungry people in town that day who didn't make it to the picnic; I hope the leftovers were shared with those who were without.

We don't know what happened to the miracle leftovers, but some of them probably made their way into *my* refrigerator. There always seem to be leftovers—and I shouldn't complain. But I'm not the only cook who feels the hardest part of cooking a meal is managing the leftovers, especially after a big holiday or company meal. Even when I declare a "leftover night" and manage to make two or three dishes of leftovers disappear, somehow a dish of leftovers remains. It takes a good deal of creativity, patience, and commitment to responsibly use up the fragments of meals when it is usually so much more tempting and interesting to cook "new" food or dishes.

One way to focus on environmental concerns is to deal responsibly with leftovers. We *can* throw away less food. Procrastination in dealing with leftovers is the biggest culprit here. There are so many things we put in the refrigerator, thinking we'll use them in a few days. We probably won't. However, if we freeze leftovers, even little scraps of vegetables, they can be used to complete an "instant meal" when we're strapped for time. Scraps of vegetables and leftover broth or bits of meat can all go into plastic bowls in the freezer, and in winter you can toss them in a tasty soup. The key to finding and using leftovers is always labeling them, or they'll wait forever.

We've included a few recipes in this chapter that can help you use up some of those forever leftovers. Expensive scraps of leftover pork or beef can become a delicious barbecue when chopped and blended with a good sauce. Chicken leftovers make great chicken salad, chicken croquets, or lightly sautéed patties, or they can be used in any of myriad chicken casserole dishes. I usually keep even the tiniest scraps of leftover taco meat or chili soup in the freezer to use in a quick quesadilla or on a grilled hot dog. Stale bread and buns can be kept frozen in a large bag and chopped for stuffing, strata (see the recipe in this chapter), or bread pudding, if your family eats those.

Doris Longacre wrote that "soup making is collecting the odds and ends—cleaning out the refrigerator, going through the cupboards, finishing off the garden. Leftover soup is generally no problem. It is reheated next day at lunch, or poured into someone's thermos. Most soups freeze well and many actually improve with reheating."[3]

Every household should have a container in the freezer where you always throw the small leftover portions of vegetables that you never know what to do with. In the *More-with-Less Cookbook*, Helen Peifer and Joann Smith suggest adding anything that might be good in soup: leftover noodles, broth, meat, vegetables. "When the container is full, add water, perhaps more broth and seasonings and cook everything together. Each soup is always different."[4]

Here are more saving tips on what to put into soups, summarized from *More-with-Less*:

- Cook off your beef and ham bones, and turkey and chicken carcasses and bones to make tasty and nutritious meat stock for the basis for many soups or stews. Don't be shy about asking your grocery store for such bones.

- In your blender, whirl almost any leftover vegetable with a little milk to form the base of a cream soup. Simply add more milk; heat it and season to taste, and the soup is ready. The blended vegetable usually provides enough thickening. If not, stir in a bit of white sauce, which is easy to make yourself; most comprehensive cookbooks have recipes for white sauce using flour, water, and shortening.

- Your blender can also turn a leftover chicken-noodle casserole into a good stand-in for cream of chicken soup.

- Blend leftover macaroni and cheese to make a thick cheese sauce.

- Use leftover baked beans for bean soup.

- Peanut butter is also a good thickener when used in peanut soup recipes.

- Dry out celery leaves, which are usually thrown out, in a napkin-lined basket in a warm spot in the kitchen. When dry, crumble into a jar and keep on hand for soups.

For even more tips, check out the newer companions to *More-with-Less*, also from Herald Press: *Simply in Season* (2005) by

Cathleen Hockman and Mary Beth Lind; *Extending the Table* (1991) by Joetta Handrich Schlabach; and *Saving the Seasons: How to Can, Freeze, or Dry Almost Anything* (2010) by mother-daughter team Mary Clemens Meyer and Susanna Meyer. Another good comprehensive standby cookbook from Herald Press with all kinds of tips, including for leftovers and food preservation is Esther Shank's *Mennonite Country-style Recipes and Kitchen Secrets* (1987), which she wrote in part to give her three daughters everything they needed to know about cooking.

● ● ● ● ● ● ● ● ● ●

In its March 3, 2010, issue, *Scientific American* reported that the U.S. Department of Agriculture estimates that Americans throw away about 25 percent of their food.[5] I'm guessing that includes all the food wasted in our school systems from kindergarten through college. A blurb in *Christian Century* cited another study at the University of Arizona estimating that the average family of four tosses out 590 dollars worth of food each year, or about ten dollars worth a week.[6] How carefully we clip and use coupons to save a few bucks, and then throw those savings away. It is a waste not only of food, but also of the resources that went into producing it.

God's wonderful gift of food is a terrible thing to waste. God's beautiful earth is too precious to squander in litter and refuse. On the other hand, there comes a time when the only safe and sane thing left to do with leftovers is give them to the dog (yes, we feed table scraps—minus small bones—to the dog, and she is perfectly healthy), or return them to the earth through a compost pile. If you're an apartment dweller, consider vermi-composting (composting with worms), or ask your landlord to support a growing movement of adding compost options to the trash disposal system.

Finally, be alert and open to new and creative ideas. When one of my daughters studied in Leuven, Belgium, in 2002, her university attracted local media attention for its experiment in keeping a small coop of chickens in back of student apartments—in the city. The students fed the chickens their table scraps, and the chickens supplied the students with eggs. Today urban chicken coops are a growing phenomenon in some North American cities as well.

It can be fun not only to eat good wholesome food but also to be conscientious in the ways we prepare, save, and consume food.

●　●　●　●　●　●　●　●　●　●

Homemade Vegetable Beef Soup

Melodie Davis

When I first tried to make "stew" as a newlywed, I cooked beef, cabbage, potatoes, and carrots, which was my mother's way of making stew. It was delicious. My husband, however, found it severely lacking in some essential soup ingredients. My children learned to love this recipe, with adaptations: One doesn't like the macaroni, so I would set aside some of the soup before adding that. Another never liked limas, so she takes those out. My husband, bless him, says, "It is not soup without the limas and peas." Any of these items and quantities can be adapted to your family's own likes and dislikes. This recipe is great for ridding the freezer or fridge of leftover anything. It makes a huge amount; halve it if you want, or consider freezing part of it for a quick meal another night.

1 pound / 500 g beef stew meat (any kind of beef in small cubes)
1 tablespoon oil
3 large potatoes
3 carrots
1 large onion
½ head cabbage
2 stalks celery

2 quarts canned tomatoes

2 cups / 500 ml water (or as needed; you can dissolve chicken or
   beef bouillon in it if you like)

2 teaspoons salt, or to taste

1 teaspoon pepper

1–2 quarts / 1–2 L vegetables, leftover, frozen, or canned (corn,
   peas, green beans, lima beans, carrots, etc.)

1 cup / 250 ml macaroni noodles

In a large pan, brown stew meat in oil, 5–10 minutes. While that's browning, chop potatoes in small cubes, slice carrots and celery, chop cabbage. Set aside. Add tomatoes and then all raw vegetables to the meat. Add water, salt, and pepper. Bring to a boil, then simmer for 30–40 minutes. Stir in leftover or frozen vegetables, and return it to a simmer. Add macaroni, and cook another 20 minutes or so. Stir frequently to keep macaroni from sticking. When carrots are soft, everything should be done.

More options: Add any or all of the following seasonings: a bay leaf or two, garlic powder, a pinch of chili powder, oregano, marjoram, parsley.

Cheese and Vegetable Strata

Jodi Nisly Hertzler

Cheese stratas are a great way to use up leftover or stale bread. In my freezer I have an enormous bag filled with mostly heels (which my kids often refuse to eat). Traditional stratas are made by buttering slices of (usually white) bread and layering them with cheese and pouring an egg-milk mixture over it all. I don't think that method works as well with the whole wheat crusty heels that I'm usually dealing with. Plus, that's a lot of butter. So here's another, healthier method, one that is versatile—you can use any combination of cheeses or vegetables, leftover or otherwise. This can be a time saver on rushed days, too, because you can make it the night or morning before.

1 large onion, chopped

2 tablespoons olive oil

1 teaspoon salt

½ teaspoon black pepper

1/4 teaspoon freshly grated nutmeg

1 (6-oz) / 180 g package spinach, chopped (or a 10-oz / 300 g bag
   of frozen spinach, thawed and squeezed dry)

2–3 cups / 500–750 ml vegetables, diced (bell peppers, zucchini,
   summer squash, broccoli, etc.)

8 cups / 2 L cubed (1 inch) bread

3–4 cups / 750 ml–1 L cheese, grated (consider smoked cheeses,
   parmesan, cheddar, Swiss)

2½ cups / 625 ml milk

9 large eggs

2 tablespoons Dijon mustard

Cook onion in oil in a large skillet over moderate heat, stirring until soft, 4–5 minutes. Add ½ teaspoon salt, 1/4 teaspoon pepper, and nutmeg. Cook while stirring, 1 minute. Stir in remaining vegetables, and sauté just until tender and the spinach is wilted. Remove from heat.

Spread half of bread cubes in a buttered 9x13-inch baking dish and top evenly with half of the vegetable mixture. Sprinkle with half the cheese. Repeat. (You can also use 2 square dishes, and freeze or give one to a sick friend, new parents, etc.)

Whisk together milk, eggs, mustard, and remaining ½ teaspoon salt and 1/4 teaspoon pepper in a large bowl, and pour evenly over strata. Chill strata, covered with plastic wrap, at least 8 hours (for bread to absorb the milk and eggs).

Let strata stand at room temperature 30 minutes. Preheat oven to 350° F / 180° C. Bake strata, uncovered, in middle of oven until puffed, golden brown, and cooked through, 45–55 minutes. Let stand 5 minutes before serving.

Option: Add cooked and crumbled bacon, sausage, or ham.

Chicken Taco Filling

Carmen Wyse

This is a recipe I created as a way to use leftover chicken (I had made the Chicken BBQ recipe from chapter 8). The veggies called for are what work for me. But any can be left out if you don't have them on hand, and others can easily be added in. Hot pepper flakes can also be added if you like it hotter.

1–2 cups / 250–500 ml cooked chicken
1 onion, chopped
5 garlic cloves, minced
2 teaspoons cumin
1 teaspoons chili powder
1 14-ounce / 420 g can diced tomatoes
1 14-ounce / 420 g can black beans, drained and rinsed
1 bell pepper, chopped
1–2 cups / 250–500 ml corn
2–3 green onions, chopped
Salt and pepper to taste

Sauté onions, spices, and garlic until soft. Add the rest of the ingredients and simmer until most of the liquid is absorbed, about 20–30 minutes. Serve on hot tortillas topped with cheese, hot sauce, or salsa, and sour cream.

Toasted Coconut Rice Pudding

Carmen Wyse

½ cup / 125 ml cream
1½ cup / 375 ml milk
1½ cup / 375 ml leftover precooked brown or white rice
2 eggs
¼ cup / 50 ml sugar
1 teaspoon vanilla
½ teaspoon salt
½ cup 125 ml toasted coconut*

Preheat oven to 350° F / 180° C. In a medium saucepan, heat the milk, cream, and rice, stirring frequently so the milk doesn't burn. Bring just to a boil.

In a separate large bowl, combine eggs, sugar, and vanilla. Temper the egg mixture by adding a couple of spoonfuls of the rice mixture, stirring after each, then pour the egg mixture into the saucepan. Stir to combine, then stir in the toasted coconut. Pour into a buttered 1.5-quart / 1,500 ml baking dish or 9x9-inch casserole, and bake for 20 minutes. Allow to cool slightly before serving.

*Toast coconut in a cast-iron or other skillet over medium-low heat, tossing frequently until golden brown.

Suggestion: Instead of toasted coconut, add 1/3 cup of raisins and 1/3 teaspoon cinnamon.

Spaghetti Pie

Jodi Nisly Hertzler

This is a great use for leftover spaghetti, linguini, or angel hair pasta. This recipe makes two pies; I like to make one and freeze one for another day. It can easily be halved if you don't have that many leftover noodles, and the quantities can be played with. We came up with this rather different method when my husband complained about my old recipe being too dry. If you're in a hurry, skip the parmesan béchamel sauce (a French white sauce) layer, but you'll be missing out a little.

Pasta:
4–5 cups / 1–1.3 L spaghetti, angel hair, or other cooked pasta
2 eggs, beaten
1 cup / 250 ml ricotta cheese (low-fat is fine)
½ cup / 125 ml parmesan cheese, shredded
½ teaspoon dried parsley (or ½ tablespoon fresh)
½ teaspoon dried oregano (or ½ tablespoon fresh)

Mix the eggs, cheeses, and herbs together in a bowl, and dump it over the noodles, tossing to coat. Set aside.

Parmesan béchamel sauce:
3 tablespoons butter
3 tablespoons flour
1½ cup / 375 ml milk
½ teaspoon salt
⅛ teaspoon pepper (white, if you have it)
½ cup / 125 ml parmesan cheese, shredded

In a small saucepan, melt the butter over medium-low heat. Add the flour and stir until smooth. Over medium heat, cook until the mixture turns a light, golden color, 5–7 minutes.

Heat the milk to almost boiling (or microwave about 3 minutes). Add the hot milk to the butter about ½ cup at a time, whisking continuously until very smooth. Bring to a boil. Cook 10 minutes, stirring constantly, then remove from heat. Season with salt and pepper, then stir in the parmesan cheese gradually, until it's melted.

The pie:

Pasta, prepared as above

Parmesan béchamel sauce

2–3 cups / 500–750 ml of your favorite spaghetti sauce

1–2 cups / 250–500 ml mozzarella cheese

Preheat oven to 350° F / 180° C. Spray 2 9-inch pie pans with nonstick cooking spray (especially important if you skip the béchamel sauce). Pour half of the béchamel sauce into each pie pan. Divide pasta mixture in half and layer on top of the sauce, pressing down lightly and up the sides, leaving a bit of a hollow for the spaghetti sauce.

Spread 1 cup or so spaghetti sauce over noodles. Cover with aluminum foil and bake for 25–30 minutes. Remove foil. Sprinkle with mozzarella cheese and bake another 5 minutes or so, until cheese is melted. Let stand 10 minutes before serving.

Whatever-You-Want-It-to-Be Frittata

Jodi Nisly Hertzler

This is one of those flexible recipes that you can tailor to your tastes, the season, and the contents of your fridge. Frittatas seem complicated, but are really much easier than omelets. This one serves four or five, but you can reduce quantities to make an individual one, perfect for a tasty and filling lunch.

1–2 tablespoons olive oil
2–3 cups / 500–750 ml vegetables (anything, cooked or raw,
          though we recommend onions be part of the mix)
2–4 cloves garlic, minced
1–2 tablespoons herbs, chopped (your preference)
Salt and pepper to taste
9 large eggs, beaten until frothy
½–1 cup / 125–250 ml cheese, shredded (optional)

Heat olive oil in a 10-inch, nonstick, broiler-proof skillet over medium heat. Add vegetables, garlic, herbs, salt, and pepper. Cover and cook until vegetables are tender, stirring occasionally. (Add vegetable depending on how long it takes them to cook. For example, if you're using raw onion and leftover cooked broccoli, make sure the onion is nearly done before adding the broccoli.) If you're using chopped tomato, add it at the end, and cook about 5 minutes, until the liquid evaporates.

Pour eggs evenly over vegetables, tilting the pan to distribute evenly. Cover, reduce heat to low, and cook 10–15 minutes, until the eggs are almost set in the center. Preheat broiler.

Top with cheese, if using, and broil 3 minutes or until the eggs are set and the top is lightly browned. Slide onto a serving platter or serve out of the skillet; cut into wedges.

Some combinations we like:

- Onion, potato (sliced as thin as possible), spinach, chives or dill, cheddar

- Zucchini, red bell pepper, green onion, thyme, tomato, Swiss

- Red onion, spinach, black olives, basil, feta

- Onion, green pepper, tomato, oregano, parmesan and mozzarella

- Broccoli, red or yellow pepper, basil, green onion

13

● ● ● ● ● ● ● ● ● ●

Why You Don't Eat Ham with Your Fingers at a Banquet

I remember well the year my oldest daughter was first invited to the Academic Banquet at her middle school. It had been a tough year, probably her worst year of schooling, mainly because Michelle had transitioned from a small county elementary school into a much larger middle school in those tumultuous adolescent years. Academically, she was fine, but socially she suffered, being considered a nerd simply because she enjoyed learning. So it was not surprising when she qualified to attend the banquet and receive a nice medallion for her scholastic efforts. The school annually put on this nice candlelight awards dinner, served by waiters on plates with real utensils.

But my husband and I were a little aghast when we realized she was tackling the ham on her plate with her fingers. Oops, our efforts in parenting had apparently gone awry. Had we never covered Banquets 101? To be fair to Michelle, I'm sure our other daughters, Tanya and Doreen, did no better at that point.

I quietly told Michelle she needed to use her fork and knife. While our family had meals together most nights, I confess I had never paid particular attention to *how* our girls were getting the food in their mouths.

On the other hand, one evening in a restaurant when they were young, they were actually complimented for their behavior.

One of them had even spilled a drink, but an older couple stopped by and said, "You have such nice children."

Who, us? It had been an ordinary meal out on a Tuesday evening, using up gift certificates awarded to the kids by the school and the restaurant for good grades. But it was suddenly elevated to high celebration. Someone thought they were well-behaved! These same children were not above hitting and name calling, but here was a couple pronouncing them "nice."

The compliment made all of us bask in the glow of the kind words. The girls became, at least for the rest of the meal, truly nice. Courteous. Not wiggly and disruptive. As parents, we were sweeter to each other.

What a gift those few words were, turning a simple weekday meal into a moment of pure gold. Sometimes that is all it takes— and that's something we need to remember in relating to our own children. Compliments may produce more good behavior than constant criticism. It is this positive spirit that we hope reigns at mealtime. Somewhere along the line, children need to realize that one purpose of good table etiquette is to help "set the table," so to speak, for engaging in wholesome dinner conversation.

A campus minister at a large university told me he started cooking classes as part of his ministry because he found so many kids coming to college who didn't have any idea about how to cook because they didn't have a family dinner. But he also felt they didn't know much about the art of dinner conversation or normal table manners either.

Fast food and eating on the run diminishes "opportunities for conversation, communion, and sensuous pleasure; they thus shortchange the hungers of the soul," points out Leon R. Kass, MD, in *The Hungry Soul*.[1] Meals distracted by media turn eating into feeding. He says, "Wolfing down food dishonors both the human effort to prepare it and the lives of plants and animals sacrificed on our behalf. The habits of incivility, insensitivity and ingratitude learned at the family dinner table are carried out in the wider world, infecting all of American life."

Kass goes on to rephrase his point positively: "Self-restraint, consideration for others, politeness, fairness, generosity, tact, discernment, good taste and the art of friendly conversation—all learnable and practiced at the table—enrich and ennoble all of human life."[2]

Chef Lisa Schroeder, author of *Mother's Best: Comfort Food that Takes You Home Again*, says it well: "The dinner table is a great location for many lessons of civilization. We pass the plate, we use tongs instead of grabbing."[3]

Having company or guests helps kids brush up on table manners and on how to set a real table or prepare a buffet. Most kids enjoy learning how to set a table so that it looks like a magazine picture instead of a feeding trough. But why wait for company? Kids do best at company meals when they've had practice in sitting down politely at a table, not grabbing food, using a napkin, handling water glasses and other utensils carefully, and trying to have a decent conversation.

The high art of hospitality in Bible times is something we can learn from. The wedding at Cana, where Jesus turns water into wine (John 2:1-11), is as much a lesson about ancient hospitality as it is about faith. At a wedding to which Jesus, his mother, Mary, and his disciples were all invited, the host is running out of wine. Mary drops a hint to Jesus: couldn't he maybe do something here?

Jesus responds in the same manner that every son in the world has probably, at least once, responded to a request from Mom: he said no. He uses the word *woman* in addressing her, which in first-century Palestine was a term of endearment, a term that Jesus will later use in speaking to Mary from the cross. Jesus then explains to her that the time has not yet come for him to do miracles. Mary tells the servants that they should do whatever Jesus tells them to.

For the host, running out of wine would have been a severe embarrassment, an affront to his guests, who would have talked about the problem for weeks. It might have indicated to the townspeople that the host's resources had been stretched too thin, that he couldn't afford the wedding. A wedding celebration typically went for days, even a week, with the whole town attending, including the poor. It is easy to see how supplies under such circumstances could have run low, but it was still a terrible embarrassment for the host and the young couple. In her novel *The Road to Cana*, Anne Rice depicts brigands striking the caravan bringing the wine to the wedding, implying that no one would have run low on wine without some unusual occurrence. The point is, running out was a big deal because of the expectations of the guests.

We can use this story of Jesus not only attending a wedding celebration but also helping to rescue the hosts as an affirmation that serving and hosting others at table can be one way of sharing God's love and hospitality. When we expect guests, we prepare well, choosing according to personal style and tastes: good china or casual; sit-down meal or buffet with finger food; multiple silverware or minimal; cloth napkins and tablecloth, or paper and plastic; candles; maybe some flowers or other arrangement; a menu of favorites or special new dishes. Hosting guests is a time for kids to brush up on how to set the table properly, put on good manners, and politely try new foods without complaint.

In the old days, children were to be "seen and not heard" at the table. Frankly I've always thought that is an awful rule, and today I gratefully invite the full participation of children in family discussions. That's the whole point of eating together, right? Teresa, a friend from church, told me that when her children were small, they would always hop down from the dinner table as soon as they were finished eating. "We wanted them to engage in conversation a little more. We started a policy of having each one tell something about their day before they left the table. Now it has gotten to be a tradition—something they just do."

What can we expect today in the way of manners? Do you allow texting, updating status via cell phone to Facebook, playing digital games, watching television? I think it is reasonable to expect at a normal meal that neither kids nor parents interrupt the meal to send or receive a text. However, I would hope for grace in emergencies—when, for example, someone is picking up a child in ten minutes for a carpool and there is a last-minute connection to be made.

If you do like watching the evening news and it conflicts with your dinner schedules, recording the program and watching it later can be one solution. Or, if you enjoy watching the news together while eating, turn the volume down during the commercials and talk about what you have heard—if you can do so without getting into an argument about your different viewpoints.

Let's be honest. Many a meal is ruined when family members argue about politics. Or when parents tackle a tough issue with kids or reprimand a preschooler. Perhaps some of us avoid family meals precisely because of bad memories associated with prayers that become sermons on behavior: "Dear God, we pray that Lorie and David will not hit each other tonight." Perhaps we're afraid of subtle or not-so-subtle putdowns or of a wife or husband or teen storming off in hurt or anger. These things are going to happen.

But just because an argument or discipline session erupts one night doesn't mean that has to be the norm. If it is the constant companion at dinner, then issues need to be confronted and dealt with through counseling, talking with a friend or pastor, or talking with each other in a calmer and neutral setting. Fostering good table conversation also sometimes means working on discipline and table manners at a time other than mealtime.

Can parents receive phone calls but not kids? There should not be a double standard. For most of us (pastors and physicians excepted), most phone calls are not true emergencies and can wisely be left to go to voice mail. But again, there are times when exceptions must be made.

How children handle food is another matter. In our fast-food culture, so many meals are consumed on the run, with no utensils in sight. Most of us enjoy party foods or hors d'oeuvres, tapas or finger foods (recipes below), but children can be taught when to use fingers and when to use eating instruments.

But I didn't quite manage to teach that lesson before my oldest reached middle school, did I? I've laughed many times over my own almost-breach of manners in this department. When the children were small, I often ate leftovers from their plates out of habit, including in restaurants. One day at a church potluck, an adult sitting next to me had left a tasty morsel on his plate. I caught myself—just in time—reaching for his leftover.

What if I had nibbled off the plate of my boss or work colleague at an important business luncheon? No wonder my daughter picked up the ham with her fingers!

●　●　●　●　●　●　●　●　●　●

Hot Tamale Pie

Sheri Hartzler

I have made this recipe so many times I can barely read the ingredients off my card. This dish freezes well and works nicely when you need a main dish for a party but don't especially want sandwiches. I usually double the recipe, and put one dish in the freezer for the next party.

¼ pound / 50 ml ground beef
1 onion, diced
2 garlic cloves, minced
2 cups / 500 ml thick tomato sauce
1 can chili beans with liquid
¼ cup / 50 ml ripe olives, sliced or chopped
2 teaspoons olive liquid
½ teaspoon oregano
1 teaspoon chili powder
Dash Worcestershire sauce or red wine
½ pound / 250 g shredded cheddar cheese
Corn tortilla chips

Preheat oven to 350° F / 180° C. Brown ground beef. Add onion and garlic, and sauté until tender. Add tomato sauce, salt, chili powder, oregano, Worcestershire sauce, and all liquids. Cook until thick. Add beans and heat. Pour into deep dish. Cover with olives and cheese. Bake 10 minutes or microwave on high until it's hot all the way through and cheese is melted. Use chips to dip.

Mango Salsa

Carmen Wyse

I grew up in Peru, where mangos were plentiful. Later in life, I did voluntary service in San Antonio, Texas, where salsas are popular. It seemed only right to merge mangos and salsas. I've since seen many different variations on a mango salsa. This is one I came up with—very simple, flavorful, and colorful, just right for a fiesta!

3 mangos, peeled and chopped
½ red onion, diced
5 tomatillos, skinned, washed, and chopped
¼ cup / 50 ml cilantro, chopped
1 jalapeno, chopped
Juice of one lime
Salt and pepper to taste

Mix together and serve with chips.

Cheese Ball

Kimberly Metzler

A good friend from church would often share this cheese ball with us. I enjoyed it so much, I asked her for the recipe.

8 ounces / 240 g cream cheese
½ teaspoon Accent, Monosodium Glutamate (MSG)
2 tablespoons fresh chives, chopped
3 ounces / 90 g chipped beef or ham, chopped
1 cup / 250 ml Colby cheese, grated
1 teaspoon garlic powder
1 teaspoon onion powder
½–1 cup / 125–250 ml chopped nuts

Mix all ingredients except chipped beef and nuts in a mixer. Add meat and stir until well combined. Roll in chopped nuts. Refrigerate. Serve with crackers.

Pear and Prosciutto Rounds with Goat Cheese and Walnuts

Carmen Wyse

An elegant, tasty, yet simple hors d'oeuvre.

Ripe, firm pears, such as Bosc
1 lemon, juiced
Thin sliced prosciutto
Goat cheese
Walnuts
Honey

Slice the pears into disks about ⅛- to ¼-inch thick. For the disks that have seeds, cut out around the seeds with a spoon, making a donut shape, but keeping the hole as small as possible. Brush a bit of lemon juice on each disk to keep them from turning brown. Place a small mound of prosciutto on each disk. Top with several bits of goat cheese and a walnut half or several walnut pieces. Drizzle with a little honey, and serve.

Crostini Appetizers

Jodi Nisly Hertzler and Carmen Wyse

Crostini:
1 baguette, sliced thin
Garlic cloves, cut in half
Olive oil
Salt

Toast the slices of bread under a broiler until they are golden on both sides. Gently rub the toasts on one side with the cut side of a garlic clove, then brush with olive oil. Sprinkle lightly with salt (optional). Serve these toasts with a wedge of brie or other soft cheese, or top with a tapenade or another spread. Here are three of our ideas:

Sundried Tomato and Pesto Topping:

Spread each crostini with pesto (pesto recipe in chapter 14), lay a sundried tomato on top, and top with mozzarella cheese (fresh, if available). Put under the broiler or in a 450° F / 230° C oven just until cheese melts.

Creamy Parmesan Topping:

Combine 1 cup freshly grated parmesan cheese with 3–4 tablespoons milk (it should make a thick paste). Add a pinch of cayenne, ¼ cup of minced fresh parsley, and salt, if necessary. Spread on crostini. Put under a broiler until the topping is hot and melted.

Summer Tomato Basil Salad:

Stir together chopped fresh tomatoes, basil, and diced red onion. Drizzle with olive oil and salt as needed. Let sit at room temperature. Add small cubes of fresh mozzarella, if you like. Serve alongside crostini, spooning salad onto the toasts as you eat (don't put it together ahead of time, or the crostini will get soggy).

Two-Ingredient Fruit Dip

Kimberly Metzler

My sister often shares recipes with me that she loves. This is one of them.

Mix together:

1 jar marshmallow cream

8 ounces / 240 g cream cheese (softened)

Refrigerate. Serve with cut-up fruit.

Icy Holiday Punch

Kimberly Metzler

This recipe makes entertaining fun! Try orange-flavored gelatin for Thanksgiving, red or green for Christmas. (Adapted from Taste of Home 2000 *recipe)*

In a 4-quart freezer proof container, dissolve:

1 (6-oz.) / 180 g package of gelatin in 2 cups / 500 ml boiling water

Add ¾ cup / 175 ml sugar, stirring to dissolve completely

Add:

46 ounces / 1 kg plus 14 g pineapple juice

6 cups /1.5 L cold water

Freeze mixture. Remove 4 hours before serving, and add 2 liters of chilled ginger ale or 7-up. Makes 32–36 servings.

14

• • • • • • • • • •

Waiting for the "Ping":
The Joys of Preserving Foods

At our office is an old snack vending machine. It is positively a museum piece, including three "demo" snacks on display in the window: packages of Oreo-like cookies, a gooey oatmeal cookie, and peanut butter bars.

Some of us estimate that the snacks have been there ten to fifteen years. The machine is still sitting there because the vending company didn't want that particular model back. It is on the second floor of our building, so it would require a hefty moving operation to just junk it. Years ago, management posted a sign warning people *not* to buy anything out of the machine.

The amazing thing is that the snacks have not visibly deteriorated in the dozen-plus years. Sure, they are wrapped and sealed in cellophane packaging of some sort, but they have not become moldy, buggy, or gray. I'm sure they taste like cardboard—some would argue they did to begin with—or are as hard as bricks. But they look fine.

That's scary. And I suspect we all regularly eat similar foods so laced with mega-preservatives that they would probably look fine ten years from now too. This is *not* the kind of food preservation we'll be addressing in this chapter.

Take an ordinary apple that we think of as fresh, preservative-free food. My husband's cousin, who has an orchard in North Carolina, speaks with a drawl like that of comedian Jeff Foxworthy. He once reflected on the misconception that apples are healthy just because they're apples. First, he said, you treat the ground underneath the tree through fertilizer and possibly pest control. Then, through chemical spraying, you treat the apple buds while they are dormant, again when the buds break, and yet again after the petals have fallen off. Later you will probably spray to control moths, fungus, or maggots. When the apples are finally ripe, they are washed to remove not only the dirt and chemical residue but also the apple's natural "wax," so that a new wax can be applied to protect and shine. "And you thought an apple a day was supposed to keep the doctor away," he concluded with a grin.

Of course this is overstating the case. The waxes that are applied, for example, are made from natural sources. Some organic fertilizers and sprays can be used. And the website of the U.S. Apple Association, not surprisingly, defends apple-growing practices: "There is a far greater health risk from not eating fruits and vegetables than from any theoretical risk that might be posed by consuming trace amounts of pesticide residues that might be found on those foods."[1] But overall, the cousin's point is a good one: treated foods must be handled with care, and sometimes health foods are not as healthy as you think.

●   ●   ●   ●   ●   ●   ●   ●   ●

During summer and fall, many homemakers in rural areas can and freeze fruits and vegetables, making it possible to "eat local" all year, or most of the year. My environmental-science-major daughter made me more aware of the ways I don't do a good job of eating locally. I always like to keep bananas and apples on hand, even when they have to be shipped from thousands of miles away. I could do better.

Not long ago, she went out picking berries along the road and cherries from a neighbor's tree—as much as she could find so she could eat fruits in season and freeze the rest to use later. Since we don't raise our own broccoli and cauliflower (too wormy in my experience), she pushed us to avoid these California-raised veggies in summer. She encouraged us instead to eat green beans as long as the plants kept bearing, even if we were tired of them.

There's a word for those who specialize in eating locally: *locavores*. Most of us can make some changes to do better in this department. When I was growing up, eating locally was our lifestyle, but we didn't know it. It is hard for me to recognize how fortunate I was to grow up learning how to garden and can. During summer, our evening meal was usually simple: nutritious bread, milk, and whatever fruit was in season, supplemented with a side sandwich of meat and cheese and maybe some lettuce or tomato. Our main meal of the day was prepared at noon—a typical farmer meal of meat, potatoes, vegetable, salad, bread, and dessert. So we ate much lighter in the evening.

This farm tradition of making a meal out of bread and milk plus strawberries, peaches, raspberries, blackberries, or blueberries wasn't progressive for the times; it was just what you did. You ate the good gifts God gave you from your farm, garden, or orchard. You didn't go to town to buy what you didn't have.

That can be a reminder for these harder times when gas is precious and polluting. If you don't have a garden, visit the local produce stands or farmers markets, even if they're a bit more expensive. Walk or cycle if you can, and accomplish several goals at once. If your area has a Community Supported Agriculture (CSA) program, sign up. CSAs involve a subscription plan with a local grower, who delivers boxes of fresh produce in season—whatever his or her garden produces.

Children raised working in gardens soak up wonderful insights about food, gardening, preserving, and the origins of foods. They don't realize they know what they know. Some years ago, Michelle was at her friend's house, where they grew a few tomato plants in a flowerbed. Michelle proceeded to sucker off the middle growth in the Y formed by the tomato's new branch.

"What are you doing?!" her friend yelled, aghast. Michelle tried to explain the benefits of pruning off this extra growth to allow more strength to go to the development of tomatoes.

She probably should have explained the suckering issue or asked permission first, but her heart was in the right place.

Children grow up learning how to can and blanch veggies and fruit for freezing, too, if you practice food preservation. Most children love stuffing beans in cans or helping to push tomatoes or apples through a sieve to make tomato juice and applesauce. They can even learn to appreciate the peculiar smell of green beans being canned in a home canner. For me, that smell evokes thoughts of home and family—not a *pleasant* smell like a fragrance, but simply unique.

I discovered how evocative that scent is for me the year after we moved to a new home, when I processed my first canner of green beans there. As the jars sat cooling on the counter, I waited for them to "ping" as they cooled and sealed so that I could finally crawl exhausted into bed.

That distinctive smell came wafting back to our bedroom. I thought, "*Now* this really seems like home." One of my daughters also confessed to liking the weird aroma of canning beans—I think for the same reason. It evokes harvest season, home, hearth, love, relationships.

● ● ● ● ● ● ● ● ●

Several days after the terrible events of September 11, 2001, my husband's family dug potatoes in his dad's garden, which we all helped to plant and harvest. Somehow it was therapeutic to engage in that earthy labor with time to reflect on the horrible events of the week. Since my older two daughters were at college then and couldn't help with what was one of their favorite fall chores, we gathered extended family, including a three-year-old great-niece and a two-year-old great-nephew, to help with the job.

When my husband used the potato plow to unearth the goods, the potatoes spilled out on all sides of the furrow like a brown Niagara Falls. It was fun trying to generate excitement and enthusiasm by squealing with exaggerated delight when the plow unearthed its gold, so that the children would get excited too. The cousins pounced on the orbs as eagerly as if they had been Easter eggs. It wasn't hard to be enthused: a fifty-pound bag of seed potatoes had yielded about forty-five bushels for our four households, with some to share with others and a few to sell.

That reminds me of a story sent by a reader of my Another Way newspaper column. Irvin Goertzen wrote, "Our oldest son was helping me hoe potatoes with a toy hoe. After showing him which were weeds and which were potatoes, we worked side by side and talked about having some good potatoes from those plants at a meal sometime. After awhile he stopped and said to me, 'I guess we didn't plant any gravy this year, did we?'"

I like harvesting potatoes because there is little that must be done to preserve them and because they produce such a big yield. By contrast, picking, shelling, and freezing peas is labor intensive, and you end up with four pints of peas for hours of work.

Potatoes have gotten a bad rap as fattening, but they are quite nutritious—except maybe in their best-known form as fries. The potato first traveled to Europe from South America, and then, like the tomato, made its way back west to North America. Today it is a staple in many countries, ranking with rice, wheat, and maize. Long before Moses parted the Red Sea, potatoes were being grown by the Incas in the Andes. And three thousand varieties exist. These facts come from Wally Kroeker, whose father pioneered the production of corn and seed potatoes in Manitoba. Today Kroeker Farms is one of the largest potato producers in Manitoba. Kroeker adds that potatoes consume less energy from the soil than the production of wheat, and they contain an enzyme that serves as a natural anti-depressant.[2]

Scientific facts aside, I know that nothing beats the taste or simplicity of homemade mashed potatoes, a plain old baked potato including the skin (under which most of the potassium and iron lies), or a mess of potato wedges baked in a bit of olive oil and seasoning salt in the oven or on the grill.

●   ●   ●   ●   ●   ●   ●   ●   ●   ●

In Bible times, people didn't know about our modern canning or freezing methods, but they did know about eating and processing locally. Grapes were harvested and made into wine that was stored in stone jars or wineskins made from preserved animal hides. And flour for making bread was kept in its original wheat grain form, and then ground fresh as needed. My friends who grind their own flour say that freshly ground whole wheat flour can be used in greater, more wholesome proportions in homemade bread because it is fresher and doesn't make the bread so hard, a testament to the natural food preservation that people in other times practiced.

These simple foods are still used after all these centuries and across all cultures to remember Jesus' gift of himself to the world. Through the central elements of bread and wine—food that we can see, touch, taste, and smell—the ritual of communion, or the Lord's Supper, produces a holy moment for those who partake.

Jesus' description of the significance of this meal is recorded in Luke 22:19-20: "And he took bread, gave thanks and broke it, and gave it to them, saying, 'This is my body given for you; do this in remembrance of me.' In the same way, after the supper he took the cup, saying, 'This cup is the new covenant in my blood, which is poured out for you.'"

If we believe that God's Spirit is refreshed in us each time we partake, then it is literally a way for us to be connected with the Holy Spirit of the Divine as we savor the earthy taste from wheat to bread, the fruity taste from vine to wine. It is where body and spirit meet, heaven and earth connect. We remember Jesus' sacrifice of himself. Our faithful response to Christ's command—that we remember him with bread and grape—becomes part of the miracle of how God's Spirit is refreshed in us through communion.

The Lord's Supper is also usually a community celebration, and we are reminded of how we are to love each other. As we consume the communion elements, we can also taste, swallow, and absorb this spirit of Christian love.[3]

For Christians, communion can also be a reminder of how we ought to slowly savor each morsel we take into our mouths at every meal or snack, producing a much more reverent approach to the food we eat—gifts of the animal and plant kingdoms. Such mindful eating usually results in slower, healthier eating, rather than frenzied feeding. It compels us to pause for grace before each intake of nourishment. In the midst of plenty, we need whatever reminders we can draw on to appreciate the bounty. Food elevated to sacrament reminds us of the precious gift of all life.

● ● ● ● ● ● ● ● ● ●

My baby boomer generation was formed by the stories of the deprivation of the Great Depression, World War II suffering, and the Holocaust. We didn't experience those terrible realities, but our grandparents and parents made sure we heard about them more often than we wanted. My husband's aunts told me they remember their mother sometimes saying she had no idea what she would make for supper, and not because she was just tired of that daily chore. It was because there was no real food in the house. So his family and mine were brought up preserving food. I'm thankful for that legacy.

In the days after September 11, 2001, many of us wondered if the world would be plunged into World War III. Indeed, the years since have seen too much fighting and bloodshed, more terrorism, and for some, recession and loss of jobs. Times of hardship, loss, and tragedy always make us more mindful and more appreciative of what we do have.

Rows of preserved vegetables, fruits, pickles, jams, soups, and even meats that lined the basement or pantry shelves of our grandmothers were a comforting assurance that, no matter how tough times got, "my family always had food on the table," as my father-in-law frequently said.

And so today, tired but happy, we still wait for that "ping."

● ● ● ● ● ● ● ● ● ●

Homemade Condensed Cream of Chicken Soup

Jodi Nisly Hertzler

A great substitute for store-bought cans of condensed soups. This is the first recipe I've found that doesn't call for bullion, which we avoid because of the MSG. I make up this large batch and then freeze it in eight 1½-cup portions, which is the size of a typical can of condensed soup.

6 cups / 1.5 L chicken broth (homemade is best and has a richer
        flavor)
2 teaspoons poultry seasoning*
1 teaspoon onion powder
1 teaspoon garlic powder
½ teaspoon black pepper
1 teaspoon salt (or to taste, depending on how the chicken broth
        is seasoned)
1 teaspoon parsley
½ teaspoon paprika
6 cups / 1.5 L milk
3 cups / 750 ml flour

In a medium saucepan, boil chicken broth, 2 cups / 500 ml milk, and the seasonings for a couple of minutes. In a bowl, whisk together the remaining 4 cups of milk and the flour. Add it to the boiling mixture and continue whisking briskly until the mixture boils and thickens. Cool, then divide into 1½ cup / 375 ml portions, and freeze.

Variation: Instead of using onion and garlic powder, sauté diced onions and garlic in a bit of butter or canola oil until tender, and then proceed with the above recipe.

*To make your own poultry seasoning, stir together 2 teaspoons sage, 1 teaspoon marjoram, ¾ teaspoon rosemary, ½ teaspoon nutmeg, ½ teaspoon black pepper, 1½ teaspoons thyme.

Curried Green Tomato Sauce

Jodi Nisly Hertzler and Carmen Wyse

One year, in an attempt to find the perfect heirloom tomatoes, my husband cultivated 14 varieties from seed, and we filled our garden with 52 tomato plants. We knew it was too many, but we were on a quest. That summer, I canned tomatoes like I've never canned tomatoes. I had finally decided I was done with my preserving when a friend posted this recipe (which I've adapted slightly) on her blog. It was so different, I had to try it. It makes use of all those green tomatoes that don't have a chance to ripen at the end of the summer, and it's simply delicious.

3 pounds / 1.5 kg cubed green tomatoes, about 6 cups / 1.5 L
      (no peeling or coring needed)
2 onions, coarsely chopped
¼ cup / 50 ml butter or olive oil
4 tablespoons curry powder
1 tablespoon cumin
1 (14-oz.) / 420 g can coconut milk
½ cup / 125 ml brown sugar
2 tablespoons lemon juice
Salt to taste (about 1 teaspoon)

Sauté onions in butter or oil until soft. Sprinkle with curry powder and cook 3 minutes. Add remaining ingredients and simmer 30 minutes, stirring occasionally. Add more water if necessary.

Ladle into jars, seal, and process in boiling water for 30 minutes, or 10 minutes in the pressure canner. Or freeze. Makes 4–5 16-ounce jars. Serve on rice. Excellent as a main dish, or served alongside grilled chicken, fish, or pork tenderloin or chops.

Optional toppings: raisins, dried cranberries, peanuts, sunflower seeds, shredded coconut, chopped green onions, chopped apples.

Microwave Pickle

Lois Priest

This was given to me by a friend several years ago. It is the only pickle I make, because it is so easy and quick—and good too. I even chop some to put in salads. I make many batches each year, usually 30–40 pints.

3–4 cups / 750–1 L sliced cucumbers
½ cup / 125 ml green peppers, cut in strips
½ cup / 125 ml onion, cut in strips
1 teaspoon salt
½ teaspoon turmeric
½ teaspoon mustard seed
4 teaspoons celery seed
½ cup / 125 ml vinegar
1 cup / 250 ml sugar

Put sliced ingredients in large bowl. Combine spices, sugar, and vinegar, and pour over the vegetables. Stir to coat well. Cover bowl tightly with plastic wrap. Microwave for 7 minutes. Remove and place into pint jars. Seal. Makes 2 pints.

Salsa

Carmen Wyse

We got a salsa recipe off the Internet and tweaked it over the years till we finally arrived at this recipe. We often make two or three batches a year and then have plenty to use through the winter, plus some to give away. For several years we have had fresh peaches at salsa-making time; adding them makes it especially good.

21 pounds / 10 kg tomatoes, peeled, seeded, and chopped
8 pounds / 4 kg bell peppers (about 20)
4 pounds / 2 kg onions
17–20 jalapeno peppers
1 cup / 250 ml garlic (about 4 heads)
4 bunches cilantro
2 8-ounce / 240 g bottles real lime (or 8–10 limes, juiced)
1 cup / 250 ml vinegar
2 teaspoons salt
5 large cans tomato paste

Put prepared tomatoes in a 5-gallon pot. Chop peppers and onions by pulsing in the food processor, and add to tomatoes. Chop garlic, jalapenos, and cilantro in food processor and add. Add the rest of the ingredients except the tomato paste. Put some liquid from the salsa into a large bowl, and add the tomato paste to this. Whisk well and add back into the salsa. Mix well. (It works best to do this by hand—literally—but wash well afterward, especially if using a lot of jalapenos). Put salsa into clean, sterilized jars. Process in a hot water bath for 40 minutes. Makes 13–14 quarts.

Aunt Edna's Cucumber Relish

Jodi Nisly Hertzler

This recipe comes from my Aunt Edna, and it's so much better than anything you can get in the store. We use it to top hot dogs, of course, but it's also excellent for making tuna and chicken salad. Last year, we had surplus zucchini, so we tried that instead of cucumbers and couldn't tell the difference. So use either one, or a combination of the two.

4 quarts / 4 L cucumbers and/or zucchini, chopped
4 bell peppers, red or green, chopped (at least 2 red peppers—
       the color really adds something)
4 large onions, chopped
4 tablespoons salt
4 cups / 1 L sugar
4 cups / 1 L vinegar
2 teaspoons black pepper
2 teaspoons turmeric
1 teaspoon celery seed

In batches, process the cucumbers or zucchini, bell peppers, and onions in a blender or food processor until finely chopped. Dump it all in a large bowl, and stir in the salt. Let it stand for several hours (or even overnight), then drain. (Aunt Edna notes that she squeezes the water out with her hands.) Add the remaining ingredients and cook for ½ hour. Seal in jars. Makes 10–12 pints.

Pesto

Carmen Wyse

I often make up to six batches of this at a time, leaving out the parmesan and adding each batch to a large bowl until I have a whole bowl full of pesto. Then I freeze it in ice-cube trays. Once frozen, I pop them out and into a zip-close plastic *freezer bag and then put them back into the freezer to use all year. Bring out as many cubes as needed, thaw, and add the parmesan.*

3 handfuls basil leaves (about 3 cups / 750 ml)
⅓ cup / 75 ml pine nuts, almonds, or walnuts
3–5 garlic cloves
½ cup / 125 ml olive oil
⅓ cup / 75 ml parmesan cheese

Process basil, nuts, and garlic in a food processor. Stream in olive oil. Stir in parmesan.

Fresh Basil All Year Long

Carmen Wyse

A neighbor who had lived in Italy for some time gave me this tip, and I have not purchased dried basil since. Simply pick the leaves off a basil plant and place them in a zip-close plastic bag and freeze. (If you need to wash your basil to remove dirt, make sure it is thoroughly dry before freezing.) When you need basil, take out the amount needed and crumble it into your dish while it is still frozen. Although it is black, the taste is fresh and delicious.

15

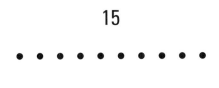

Saving Table Grace

One of the most important reasons for working hard to create time and space for regular family mealtimes is the opportunity it creates to observe regular family prayers. And one of the main causalities of a "grab it and growl supper" or the "everyone for themselves" approach to mealtime is *grace*. It is practically impossible to have prayer or to pause to recognize the giver of our food and the "hands that prepared it" in a culture where gathered mealtimes happen so infrequently.

My parents managed to have family devotions every day at breakfast, even if we were all dashing off to school. It included a reading from our devotional magazine, *Rejoice!*, a Scripture, a printed prayer request from church agencies, and prayer. Mom and Dad would take turns leading it.

Our Davis family treasured observing daily Bible readings and meditations for most of Advent and Lent. And we always practiced mealtime grace. Usually we take turns saying our own prayer; the made-up prayers of children are some of the most tender—or funniest—moments in parenting. We never got into the habit of using written prayers or memorized graces. Those are fine, but there is something wholesome about praying whatever is on your heart and mind.

One reader of my newspaper column wrote about how her son spoke volumes one day during an elongated grace. He had launched into one of his never-ending prayers that named every-thing on the table, all his favorite toys, friends, pets, and for good measure, his unfavorite foods. The family knew their Sunday din-ner was growing not only cold, but also crusty. When he was gently hurried along in his prayer by a well-meaning parent, he stopped and said, "Dad, you're not supposed to interrupt people when they're talking to God. Now I am just going to have to start over."

Luckily, by this time, he was getting hungry too, and he brought his second prayer to a quick conclusion. After micro-waving the food that had grown cold, it was a blessed reminder of how, indeed, even children shouldn't be interrupted when they're talking to God.

Keeping daily grace is something that easily falls by the way-side when young adults go off to college or move away from home, especially if their parents don't stress the importance of daily gratitude to God. When you are around people who don't pause before a meal, or you are eating on the run or in front of a laptop or video game, it is easy to forget about stopping to thank God for your food. My children all went to state universities, and prayer in those settings is rare. I went to a Christian college in the seventies, where the expectation was that you bowed your head at the dining hall table and either counted to ten or said a genuine prayer.

Why bother with grace?

- It is a counter-cultural way to proclaim your individ-ual and family Christian loyalty. This act is no longer a common, Norman Rockwell moment in homes, so continuing the practice sends an important message.
- It is a good way to focus, forcing attention away from fights, conversation, or electronic devices. It allows for time to center on God.
- It is an opportunity to verbally remember the folks you promise to pray for, even if you can't get through the whole list every night and even if you only say, "Be with Charles, and John and Martha."

- Grace can be one more way to instill an attitude of gratefulness in your family. We need frequent reminders that everything we have comes from God.
- It can be a way to express your support and care for your children as you pray about their upcoming tests, a trip, a paper, and their friends.
- Sometimes things that you do not or cannot address with eyes open and in normal conversation can be broached in prayer: "Help Susie's friends to get along." (But avoid the sermon masquerading as prayer: "Help Susie not to say bad words at the table.")
- It teaches children the practice and skill of spoken corporate prayer. Many adults do not feel comfortable praying out loud in a group. For those of us who grew up learning this skill from daily practice, praying out loud is no big deal.
- It can create tender, bonding memories for a family.

The family table grace that is indelible in my mind occurred the day my grandfather died. My grandparents lived with us in our home in separate quarters. Dad was the youngest child, and he developed an intimate bond with both parents in those later years. Grandpa lived to be ninety-two, and he weighed no more than that in his final days. The morning Grandpa died, Dad was trying to help him get a little nutrition through a drink or some food, and Grandpa ended up choking. The effort consumed him, and he passed away in Dad's arms. Dad felt terrible, but Grandpa had lived a full life, was longing to go to heaven to be with Grandma, and was ready to die.

The undertaker came to our home to retrieve Grandpa's body, and we made preliminary funeral preparations. It was summer, so we kids were not in school. At lunch, we paused for our normal blessing. It was Dad's turn to pray, and he tried to begin. But no words would come out. He was quietly sobbing, a rarity for Dad. What should we do? Our strong and hearty farmer dad was not able to lead in prayer.

It was then that Mom's quiet but sure voice took over,

praying the only prayer that came to her mind in that moment of fresh grief and numbness: "Our Father which art in heaven; hallowed be thy name; thy kingdom come, thy will be done, on earth as it is in heaven." It was a hallowed moment, a time when I was proud and thankful for my parents and our tradition of mealtime grace.

The Lord's Prayer (Matthew 6:9-13; Luke 11:2-4) is as good a prayer as any to teach to children early on. And it can be a standard mealtime grace to use while they are learning it. "Give us this day our daily bread" is a succinct reminder of how dependent we are on God for so much, including the daily gift of food. Other parts of the prayer teach the basics of daily confession and forgiveness, respect for God's name and God's being, and reliance on God for perseverance in times of trial.

The problem with repeating the Lord's Prayer or any prayer is that it can become rote and meaningless. One traditional and familiar rhyme we children did use until we outgrew it was this:

> God is great
> God is good
> Let us thank him for our food
> By his hands we all are fed
> Give us, Lord, thy daily bread. Amen.

This prayer, inspired by the Lord's Prayer, shows how variations on a theme can be helpful. Including variety and making up our own prayers keeps meaning and spontaneity in the observance.

In her precious little volume called *Peanut Butter and Jelly Prayers*, Julie B. Sevig offers some smile-inducing, funky prayers that kids and parents love. She is a mother of three, including a four-year-old at the time of the publication, and is from the Evangelical Lutheran Church in America, my husband's tradition. She offers prayers over meals for real families in our daily rush—whether it is boxed macaroni and cheese:

Boil the water
Add the noodles
Mac and cheese
We love you oodles
In gratefulness for this creation
We bow and eat with such elation.[1]

Or for a trip through the fast-food window:

We want it fast, we want it now
Thank you God, for the cow
For burgers, fries and all we chew
For all who work at this drive-thru.[2]

Sevig's prayers generally bring in some other element that lifts them beyond simple, cute poem, such as in the reminder of the plight of the workers who shovel out fast food or of those who do not have enough to eat, as in this prayer for pizza:

Bless the cheese
Bless the meat
O dear God, bless all who eat
For those who hunger, those who shiver
We thank you God—you too, deliver.[3]

And finally this for any Leftovers Night:

You've blessed these before, and you bless them again
With these our leftovers, let the feasting begin;
But please, dear Lord, when this meal is through
Let's say to what's left: *We bid you adieu.*[4]

Sevig's book includes much more: simple family prayers for all seasons of the church year and many holidays—seventy-five all together. She also offers suggestions for discussion or conversation that follow the prayer. It makes a great companion or follow-up for anyone serious about mealtime and the accompanying grace or prayer time.

Another writer, Anita L. Fordyce, says, "The family mealtime gives the opportunity for the family to be knit together in love and fellowship. When a family eats together, they make [God's] name to be remembered in all generations (Psalm 45:17)."[5]

We've probably all heard the brief fun prayer "Rub-a-dub-dub, thanks for the grub. Yea, God!" If you think that too irreverent, you can do as one family does. They add, "Bless us, O Lord, for these gifts we are about to receive from your bounty. Amen."

Some families who have good voices or at least love singing make a regular habit of singing their family grace. This is a beautiful tradition as well. Even if it is only the Johnny Appleseed song, there's something nice about uniting around a simple chorus:

> Oh, the Lord's been good to me
> And so I thank the Lord
> For giving me the things I need
> The sun and rain and the apple seed
> The Lord's been good to me.

The story behind the song is that in the 1700s, John Chapman, who became known as Johnny Appleseed, carried a sack on his back filled with apple seeds and planted them in western portions of New York and Pennsylvania. It is hard to sing the song without being lighthearted and thankful.

If your kids are familiar with Superman, you might try the "Superman" prayer song. The fun part is you stand singing it with your hands raised over your head like you are flying, gently swaying back and forth in Superman fashion:

> We thank you, Lord, for giving us food
> We thank you, Lord, for giving us food
> Our daily bread, you keep us fed,
> We thank you, Lord, for giving us food. Amen.

Another popular sung prayer with a great deal more majesty is "Great God":

> Great God, the giver of all good;
> Accept our thanks and bless this food
> Grace, health, and strength to us afford
> Through Jesus Christ, our risen Lord!

What happens to table grace when you eat out? Do you pray aloud or silently? These are questions that are personal to each individual and family. While I was sometimes embarrassed as a child when my father would make us bow our heads and pray silently while eating out, now I'm thankful for that habit he instilled. While there is a danger of making a "show" of prayer, which is discouraged in the Bible, a silent moment of prayer before a meal should be offensive to no one. I am always quietly blessed when I see others bowing their heads in a restaurant.

It is important, though, to participate in such a prayer with the right spirit: truly centering on God and expressing gratitude for the gifts of food and the people we are with. Too often we spend the silent time focusing on other preoccupations: "Okay, have I prayed long enough?" Or "Maybe people will think I'm just fixing my napkin." Or "What if the waiter comes now?" However, when we consider how much we have received from God, it is easier to put aside the surroundings and focus on truly thanking God.

Restaurant prayers have their place, especially if you eat in a secluded seating area or if the prayer is said quietly or if you are in a large family gathering. As a Christmas gift, my mother treated her nearby family members to a meal at a large Amish restaurant. My husband and I were visiting her, and my sister's family, children, grandchildren, step-children, and step-grandchildren were all there, plus her husband's mother. We had a private dining room, and before digging into the bounty, we gathered in a circle, holding hands. As I gratefully surveyed that sphere, I couldn't help thinking of the family stories that brought us all to that moment, through numerous trials and temptations and difficulties. I felt the saving grace of our Lord in that precious family circle as we joined hands while an adult grandchild led us in group prayer.

That is why the practice of prayer before meals is worth

keeping. My father, a hog farmer, used to say how uncivilized it was just to dig into a meal without praying, like pigs at a trough.

All those who work so hard to make and provide food—farmer, gardener, chef, fast-food worker, cooks at home—know the effort it takes to feed our families. Those who don't work long hours in factories, offices, or hectic schoolrooms don't work directly with food, but they provide the money to purchase the food; they, too, know what it takes to put food on the table.

Instilling an attitude of thankfulness should be a top priority in a Christian family, no matter how many times a day you practice prayer. Jesus gave thanks in a public way before he fed the crowds and in private with the disciples before his last supper. Ephesians 5:20 puts it well: "Always [give] thanks to God . . . for everything in the name of our LORD Jesus Christ."

● ● ● ● ● ● ● ● ● ● ●

Just as this book has looked at the importance of good nutrition for our bodies, so we need to pay attention to nutrition for our spiritual well-being. I have talked about how frenetic our family lives and schedules are today and would be remiss not to remind us of the importance of taking time to feed our spirits. Our lives are too often centered on self. Even our prayers are sometimes focused only on my family, my wants, my schedule.

As parents, we set an example in this too. We must teach children to be grateful and then illustrate that with our lives.

Sam Janzen, a beloved pastor in our area of Virginia, told the story of his eight-year-old grandson, who occupied his hands during a sermon Sam was preaching by doodling on a piece of paper. Sam wondered how well the boy was listening.

Sam's sermon had been about the ten men cured of leprosy in the Bible, and how only one bothered to say "thank you." Sam expounded on nine reasons why the persons with leprosy might have neglected their thanks. Perhaps, he speculated, as people with long-term illness, they had so much done for them that they simply had "run out of thank-yous."

After the sermon, Sam's grandson said to him, "I don't see how anyone could ever run out of thank-yous."

Ah, yes, son, you got it right. How could anyone ever run out of thank-yous—or not have enough time to say grace? And yet we do.

- Did I forget to thank God this morning for the gift of waking up with a healthy body?
- Did I forget to be thankful for running water in my house?
- Did I forget to thank my spouse for going to work today to help buy food for our family? Have I thanked my boss or supervisor for my job or the work he or she does?

How can we not offer thanks? How could we possibly run out of thank-yous?

Notes

Introduction

1. Joseph A. Califano Jr., "The Importance of Family Dinner V," National Center on Addiction and Substance Abuse at Columbia University, September 2009, 5, http://www.casacolumbia.org/templates/Publications_Reports.aspx.

2. Lonnie Golden and Helene Jorgensen, "Time after Time: Mandatory Overtime in the U.S. Economy," Economic Policy Institute, EPI Briefing Paper #120, January 2002, http://www.epi.org/publications/entry/briefingpapers_bp120/.

3. American Community Survey, U.S. Census Bureau, "Americans Spend More Than 100 Hours Commuting to Work Each Year, Census Bureau Reports," March 30, 2005, http://www.census.gov/newsroom/releases/archives/american_community_survey_acs/cb05-ac02.html.

4. Califano, "The Importance of Family Dinner V," 6.

5. Victoria J. Rideout, Ulla G. Foehr, and Donald F. Roberts, "Generation M2: Media in the Lives of 8- to 18-Year-Olds," Kaiser Family Foundation, January 2010, 15, http://www.kff.org/entmedia/upload/8010.pdf.

6. Califano, "The Importance of Family Dinner V," 4.

7. Cited in Allison Leach, "Secrets of a Happy Home," *Family Life*, August 1998, 65.

8. Califano, "The Importance of Family Dinner V," 5.

9. Ibid.

Chapter 1: Even Cave Kids Knew What Dinner Was

1. *World Book Encyclopedia* (Chicago: World Book, 1988), vol. 7, 336.

2. These descriptions are based on oral traditions, documented in "Table Manners: Pacific Northwest Native Americans in Olden Times," http://nativeamericans.mrdonn.org/northwest/tablemanners.html (accessed July 26, 2010).

3. "The Convivium-Social Structures in Dining," http://hubpages.com/hub/romandining (accessed July 26, 2010).

4. James Krabill, "Consultation Meals Suggest 'The Best is Yet to Come,'" *Missions Now*, Fall 2000, 10.

Chapter 2: The Family That Gardens Together Eats Together

1. Alyce McKenzie, *Parables for Today* (Louisville: Westminster John Knox Press, 2007), 44.

2. Judith Bortner Heffernan, "Our Daily Bread: The Business of Rural America," *Sojourners*, September–October 1995, http://www.sojo.net/index.cfm?action=magazine.article&issue=soj9509&article=950911.

3. Barbara Kingsolver with Steven L. Hopp and Camille Kingsolver, *Animal, Vegetable, Miracle: A Year of Food Life* (New York: HarperCollins, 2007), back cover.

Chapter 5: Comfort Food and Memories

1. "What is Comfort Food?" Intentional Simplicity, http://www.intentionalsimplicity.com/cfcb/comfortfood.html (accessed July 26, 2010).

Chapter 7: So What If Dinner Isn't Picture-Perfect?

1. Doris Janzen Longacre, *More-with-Less Cookbook* (Scottdale: Herald Press, 2000), 25.

Chapter 10: Getting Kids to Like Okra and Moo Goo Gai Pan

1. Nancy Tringali Piho, *My Two-Year-Old Eats Octopus: Raising Children Who Love to Eat Everything* (Boulder: Bull Publishing, 2009), 20.

2. Ibid., 69.

Chapter 11: Eating All Day for the Price of One Grande Caffè Latte

1. Tawra Kellam, *Dining on a Dime* (Temple, TX: T&L Group, 2004.) She is found at http://www.livingonadime.com.

2. Mitch Albom, "Music in the Rubble," *Parade*, March 28, 2010, http://www.parade.com/news/backpage/mitch-albom/100328-music-in-the-rubble.html.

3. Arvind Subramanian, "U.S. Leadership in the Global Food Crisis," Institute for International Economics, http://www.iie.com/publications/papers/paper.cfm?ResearchID=931.

Chapter 12: How Food, Packaging, and Waste Impact the Planet

1. Everything2, "50 Simple Things You Can Do to Save the Earth," http://everything2.com/index.pl?node_id=1167112.

2. Longacre, *More-with-Less Cookbook*, 23.

3. Ibid., 196.

4. Ibid., 197.

5. "Waste Land: Does the Large Amount of Food Discarded in the U.S. Take a Toll on the Environment?" *Scientific American*, March 3, 2010, http://www.scientificamerican.com/article.cfm?id=earth-talk-waste-land.

6. "What a Waste," *Christian Century*, April 6, 2010, 9.

Chapter 13: Why You Don't Eat Ham with Your Fingers at a Banquet

1. Leon R. Kass, *The Hungry Soul* (Chicago: University of Chicago Press, 1999), cited in *Utne Reader*, November–December 2000, 56.

2. Ibid.

3. Lisa Schroeder, *Mother's Best: Comfort Food that Takes You Home Again* (Newtown, CT: Taunton Press, 2009), cited in Barbara Mahany, "Family Dinner: Memories are made of this," Philly.com, January 14, 2010, http://www.philly.com/philly/restaurants/81346287.html.

Chapter 14: Waiting for the "Ping"

1. U.S. Apple Association, "Apples and Pesticide Residues," July 26, 2002, http://www.usapple.org/consumers/pesticides.cfm.

2. Wally Kroeker, *God's Week Has Seven Days* (Scottdale, PA: Herald Press, 1998), 147–49.

3. Theological reflections adapted from an email by Dr. Don Allen, founding pastor of Trinity Presbyterian Church, Harrisonburg, Virginia.

Chapter 15: Saving Table Grace

1. Julie B. Sevig, *Peanut Butter and Jelly Prayers* (Harrisburg/ New York: Morehouse Publishing, 2007), 5. Copyright © 2007 Morehouse Publishing. Used by permission.

2. Ibid., 4.

3. Ibid., 6.

4. Ibid., 12.

5. Anita L. Fordyce, "The Family that Eats Together," *Living for the Whole Family*, Fall 1999.

Recipe Index

The Authors

Melodie M. Davis grew up on a farm near Goshen, Indiana, where in summer she ate a lot of sweet corn, tomatoes, and ham, and attended a Mennonite high school, where her favorite food was homemade cinnamon rolls. Her parents were Vernon U. and Bertha Stauffer Miller: her father was famous for making barbecue chicken and her mother's claim to food fame was putting three meals on the table every day: breakfast, lunch, and supper.

Melodie graduated from high school in Blountstown, Florida, and spent one year in Mennonite Voluntary Service near Hazard, Kentucky. She graduated in 1975 from Eastern Mennonite College (now University) with a BA in English. The same year, she began working at Mennonite Broadcasts, now Third Way Media, in Harrisonburg, Virginia. Through the years, she has written and produced media for radio, television, video, Internet, and print.

Melodie has written a syndicated newspaper column since 1987, Another Way. She is also the author of ten books, including *Why Didn't I Just Raise Radishes: Finding God in the Everyday*; *Working, Mothering and Other Minor Dilemmas*, as well as *366 Ways to Peace*, a calendar. In 2010 she helped launch a new weekly radio program, *Shaping Families*, for which she serves as producer and co-host.

When Melodie and her husband, Stuart, married in 1976, her cooking practice began in earnest. Today they live near Singers Glen, Virginia, and are parents of three adult daughters, Michelle, Tanya, and Doreen. She is an ordained elder in the Presbyterian Church USA and a member of Trinity Presbyterian Church, Harrisonburg.

Jodi Nisly Hertzler lives with her husband and three children in Harrisonburg, Virginia. She works from home, answering questions sent to the Third Way Café website (www.thirdway.com), and is the author of *Ask Third Way Café: 50 Common and Quirky Questions about Mennonites.*

Early in their marriage, Jodi and her husband, Shelby, led a Service Adventure volunteer household in Oregon. Cooking and sharing meals on a tight budget kindled Jodi's interest in creating healthy meals from whole foods, a concern that grew when she became a mother. Jodi made all her children's baby food from scratch and is always on the lookout for new flavors and dishes that might appeal to the whole family.

Carmen Wyse lives in Harrisonburg, Virginia, with her husband, Wayne, and two nearly teenage sons. She holds a degree in social work and works part time for Big Brothers Big Sisters. Carmen grew up in a missionary family that ate three meals a day together. While her current lifestyle and schedules don't allow for that routine, it has not been a stretch to make evening meals together a priority.

Carmen enjoys nurturing her garden during the summer and "putting up" food for the winter. She continues to enjoy cooking and finding new, creative recipes to intersperse between the tried and true.